"So Many Bad Films... So Few Brain Cells..."

Trashfiend

Disposable horror fare of the 1960s & 1970s

Volume One

Scott Stine

www.headpress.com

Trashfiend

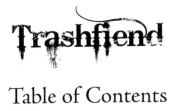

Table of Contents

Film Reviews

Appendix

IN SPRING OF 2002, I self published the first issue of *Trashfiend* under my Stigmata Press imprint, a forty eight page tribute to 'Horror & Exploitation Fare from the 1960s & 1970s.' With a modest print run of 2,000 copies, and sporting an underexposed but garish full color cover, *Trashfiend* picked up where its predecessor *GICK!* left off the previous year. Although far more comprehensive than the earlier incarnation, the primary thing that set *Trashfiend* apart was its unwavering devotion to media that left the greatest impression on me as a child. I had grown tired of more recent fare, which had become evident in the gradual decline of post 1980 coverage in *GICK!* (When I did review such films, I rarely had anything good to say about them… unless, of course, they were throwbacks to the stuff that made up the cinematic soundtrack of my youth.) If any incarnation of the magazine were to survive, I *had* to be inspired by or at least marginally interested in the material covered within its pages. Even if many of the films and comics I wrote about were, well, trash, at least it was trash that was near and dear to my heart.

In the editorial that kicked off the first issue of *Trashfiend*, I made a sincere but ultimately feeble attempt to explain the main impetus behind the magazine's conception: nostalgia. But it wasn't until I was wrapping up this book that I found myself one step closer to truly understanding the great cosmic force that makes the crustiest curmudgeons shuck their catch-all bah, humbug's and sigh in fond remembrance of days past. I was in the midst of writing the piece that closes this book, 'Sleeplessness in Seattle,' when I found myself caught up in something more than casual reminiscence. I was trying desperately to save a part of my childhood that, unlike many of the things covered in this book, was slipping through the cracks of popular history. With an unprecedented urgency, I was soon consumed by the need to archive every scrap of data and trivia about this childhood obsession that I could unearth. My previous efforts to preserve all things vintage horror paled in comparison to the machinations that drove my most recent obsession. I had discovered my grail, my ark of the covenant… even if friends and family alike thought it high time I purchase a one-way ticket to the bughouse, I felt justified.

As adults, we rarely experience the awe we took for granted as children. As we grow older, we gradually become more desperate to relive such moments, and we find that only through the very things that sparked our collective imaginations as children can we even come close to this now-elusive wonderment. For me, and probably many of the people reading this, it was monsters and everything devoted to them: films, comics, toys, movie magazines, what have you. That, of course, is a goodly part of what *Trashfiend* entails. But this beast has a particularly dark underbelly: stained and matted nether regions sullied by its need to wallow in the blood and the muck. As some of us

After seeing these examples of Rick Baker's effects work for The Incredible Melting Man (1977), this film capped my Top Ten Most Wanted list for years.
Starlog #11 (January 1978) Starlog Communications

socially acceptable fashion lest they be compared to tapeworms or other unsavory parasites that inhabit one's lower intestinal tract.

Due to its inextricable ties with these taboos, the horror genre has always shared this stigma, but never more so than during the sixties and seventies when—excuse the mixed metaphor—it pushed the envelope and exploited the inability of weary censors to assert any real control over the breached floodgates. And since the entrepreneurs who capitalized on the growing market for titillation and bloodshed produced their lurid product as cheaply as humanly possible, much of it was and is viewed as 'trash' by the general consensus. Although I would be hard pressed to consider Warren Publications or the writings of Robert Bloch and Leslie Whitten as garbage, the fact that they are horror automatically relegates them to the position of disposable entertainment in the eyes of many people. At best, horror is kid's stuff; at worst, the products of the genre are censured for fueling a savage and debauched society and regarded with utter disdain. Either way, like it or not, it's trash.

Of course, some of the films covered in *Trash-fiend* are moldering turds that should never have been disinterred, except as a target of adoring ridicule from confused individuals like myself. But the films that offer the viewer more than just an opportunity to prove their prowess as the next Joel Robinson or Mike Nelson offer something special, something unique to their respective cultures and the discombobulated decades in which they were spawned. Much of this fare displays verve, characterized by a low budget ingenuity or an unrestrained viscera that is painfully absent from anything produced in the last twenty plus years. It has heart and soul, even if it is riddled with atheromata and moral degradation.

The best of it, of course, makes some of us feel like a kid again.

grew up, the unattainable 'mature' horrors that our impressionable minds were mostly spared became our newfound sirens, our need to seek out their forbidden pleasures fueled by the very fact they were once taboo. Anything that hid behind an R rating, or was placed on the top shelf of the magazine rack beyond our adolescent reach, *had* to be something special. As horror fans, we were always looking for something new to shock our jaded sensibilities, so it was our very nature to grasp at things concerned adults did not want us to see.

Most of the things considered taboo in our society are labeled as such because they appeal to our basest nature, and they are often summed up with the lowest common denominators of sex and violence. Despite the fact these distasteful subjects are the cornerstones of American entertainment, they bear a stigma that forces respectable producers and publishers to peddle their wares in a more co-starring in the remake of The Blob sixteen years later . . . yet another earthbound disaster that should have been consumed by flames before it reached the surface. I can't help but feel a sense of relief that he passed away just before the ultimate degradation, when Beware! The Blob was rescued from obscurity by the DVD revolution.

At best, 'the film that JR shot' amounts to little more than a string of skits stripped of their punch lines. When the only suspense to be found is dependent upon whether or not some poor sap is going to plop down on a weathered recliner in which the Blob has already made itself cozy, the viewer is reminded just how short life really is.

I have to ask, in which shopping mall did you find the composer for your score? It must have been tough dragging him away from his Hammond organ, with the bustling crowds held in rapt attention and all.

However, I must congratulate your crew for a few palatable space booger effects. That is, those not conceived through forced perspective shots. Or through the reversal of the film stock. Or utilizing inflatable stand-ins. The rest isn't half bad.

I just don't get it. Are we to assume that your cameo in Beware! The Blob as a begrimed transient was indicative of your state of affairs at the time, and that taking this job was a desperate attempt to pull yourself out of the gutter? If this was the case, we could forgive such transgressions as long as you promised never to step behind a fully loaded camera again.

Please don't take this tirade as a personal attack. From all reports, you sound like a really great guy, having contributed much time and resources to some very worthy causes. But couldn't you have rested on your laurels? It's safe to say that many a boy discovered his sexuality long before puberty, thanks to I Dream of Jeannie, and thus you—Major Nelson—were cool by association and the envy of all. For this you would not be forgotten, but then you had to go muck it all up by making fun of both the sci fi genre and its aficionados by having a hand in this lousy sequel.

Jeezus, Larry . . . what were you thinking?

Sincerely, Scott Stine

P.S. Could you sign and return the enclosed photo of you as Cedric Acton from the Dec. 16, 1970, episode of Night Gallery? Thanks.

Blood and Lace (1971)

The Carlin Company [US] DIR: Philip S Gilbert PRO: Ed Carlin and Gil Lasky SCR:Gil Lasky DOP: Paul Hipp MUS: John Rons STR: Peter Armstrong, Dennis Christopher, Maggie Corey, Gloria Grahame, Len Lesser, Terry Messina, Melody Patterson, Milton Selzer, Louise Sherrill, Mary Strawberry, Ronald Taft and Vic Tayback
AKA: El Martillo Macabro [The Macabre Hammer]
      El Sotano del Terror [The Cellar of Terror]
      Visión Sangrienta [Bloody Vision]
Approximately 86m; Color; Rated GP
ADL: "Shock After Shock After Shock... As Desire Drives a Bargain with Death!"

SHOCK!
AFTER
SHOCK!
as Desire
drives a
bargain
with
DEATH!

STARRING
GLORIA GRAHAME · MILTON SELZER · LEN LESSER
VIC TAYBACK | MELODY PATTERSON | AS ELLIE | COLOR BY MOVIELAB

WRITTEN BY   ASSOCIATE PRODUCER   PRODUCED BY
GIL LASKEY · CHASE MISHKIN · ED CARLIN and GIL LASKEY · PHILIP GILBERT
GP   A CONTEMPORARY FILMAKERS/CARLIN COMPANY PRODUCTION released by AMERICAN INTERNATIONAL PICTURES

BLOOD
AND
LACE

71/69

US lobby card for Blood and Lace (1971) American International Pictures, Inc.

A WOMAN and her lover are murdered in their sleep by someone wielding a claw hammer; not much attention is given to the case, as the fairer of the two has a disreputation for being 'user-friendly,' and most of the clues are destroyed in a fire set to cover the killer's tracks. Being the only witness to the crime, the woman's daughter, Ellie Masters (Melody Patterson), is befriended by a detective assigned to the puzzling murder case, a sleazy ex-theatre owner named Calvin (Vic Tayback) who has taken time out from his busy schedule of "sniffing around for good breeding stock" to look for the culprit. Left without a mother and clueless as to the identity of her father, the teenage girl is shipped off to Deere Youth Home, an orphanage the abandoned youth of a Dickens novel would consider a summer camp.

The matron of this fine, fine establishment, the widow Mrs Dottie Deere (Gloria Grahame), is a little wiggy to say the least. In addition to sleazing her way into the heart of the doctor (Milton Selzer) whose job it is to make sure everything stays up to code, she spends her off hours filling the basement freezer with the bodies of attempted runaways and ranting about bringing people back from the dead. (Suffice to say, her very dead hubby Jameson has been spared a proper burial as well.) She is assisted by her handyman Tom (Len Lesser), a work of art who makes the slimy detective look like a saint. Soon, Ellie starts having nightmares involving her mother's torched lover, back from the dead and ready to make short work of the surviving Masters with his own Stanley whack-o-matic.

In my early teens, a ratty one-sheet poster for this film adorned my bedroom wall, my reverence assured even having never seen it. (During my youth, *Blood and Lace* showed up on *Nightmare Theatre*—undoubtedly cut—but I was apparently indisposed the night it aired. It's safe to assume that even truncated this film would have left a lasting impression on my delicate psyche.)

When I finally acquired a third generation copy of *Blood and Lace* just a few years back, I was not disappointed... except for one thing, something that still vexes me to this very day. Namely, this: where in Sam Hill is the claw hammer killer sporting sunglasses and a lavender robe? This androgynous psychopath graces every piece of ad art ever used for the film, both domestic and abroad, yet proves to be *in absentia* once the film rolls. I've grown very accustomed to the unfulfilled hyperbole that dominates advertising for trash horror from the sixties and seventies—hell, I live for it, knowing full well that the films can rarely live up to such great expectations—but discovering that this purple hooded hammer wielding sociopath was nothing more than the fever dream of a bored advertising executive has left me feeling unfulfilled.

In addition to The Perplexing Case of the Misplaced Mascot, *Blood and Lace* offers numerous mysteries... the most prominent being that it was released upon an unsuspecting public with a GP [General Public] rating. Although it is probably a stretch, one can't help but wonder if this production was singlehandedly responsible for the MPAA [Motion Picture Association of America] replacing the ambiguous GP with a far more pointed PG [Parental Guidance] the following year. That aside, even the more liberal filmgoers like myself recognize *Blood and Lace* as a clearcut case for an R rating. (Heck, it's a clearcut case illustrating just why we established a ratings board in the first place.)

Granted, much of the sex and violence is only implied, but had they shown exactly what was going on off-screen, most theatregoers would have found the film unbearable. Surprisingly, there is no nudity, and the bloodshed is negligible (a runaway's hand being hacked off with a meat cleaver being the only bit of graphic bloodletting); it is instead the implied necrophilia, the potentially incestuous situations, the attempted teen rape and molestation, the Nazi-esque torture tactics and what have you, that makes it a tasteless excursion. Heck, the lurid tone that permeates the script is enough to get the film slapped with a far more restrictive rating if it ever gets a legit video release. *Henry—Portrait of a Serial Killer* couldn't secure an R in 1987 because of its bleak atmosphere, and it's not nearly as scummy as this modest flick, made sixteen years previous.

Like McNaughton's piece de resistance, *Blood and Lace* also brims with unsavory characters in the midst of perpetrating unsavory acts, but here it is cheap and tawdry instead of artistic and thought provoking. (Although there is a somewhat somber moment when—having been confronted with the bloody fates of their peers and given the opportunity of escape—the troubled teens stand numbly instead of beating their feet, the oldest among them asking, "But where do we go?") And lest we forget the finale, which only emphasizes the sensational-minded script: neither of the revelations saved for the last act are particularly unexpected, but they make for a double whammy of a downbeat climax to what has already proven a downright downbeat film.

Technically, the film is just as gritty; it wouldn't surprise me in the least to discover that *Blood and Lace* was shot over a weekend using borrowed equipment. The overbearing soundtrack—pilfered classical music broken on occasion by a troubled theremin—is often used to great effect in distracting the viewer from the rugged produc-

Mexican lobby card for Blood and Lace (1971) Rozil Distribuidor

tion values. One of the areas in which the production would have benefited from a couple of extra bucks is the makeup department. Enter the vengeful apparition of the nameless John killed alongside Ellie's mother. Many films have used scarred killers to good effect, but our heroine's assailant looks like an old man who fell asleep at the breakfast table and took a face plant into his bowl of oatmeal.

Blood and Lace and the people involved demonstrate ingenuity on at least one occasion, though. I am, of course, speaking of the film's patented claw hammer cam. Too lazy to have the cameraman hold a murder weapon in front of the lens as he plays the part of a psychopath sneaking up on the intended victims? No problem. Simply attach the tool to an immobile extension from the camera rig, and voila! Claw hammer cam. Sure,

it robs entire scenes of anything even remotely resembling tension, but the viewer is simply too awed by the awkward gimcrackery to care.

Not enough tease? We have a teenage catfight involving sleepwear, after one of them successfully seduces the other's boyfriend. Not enough splatter? In one of the film's most effectively shocking moments, we are offered a loving close up of a defrosting corpse's seeping stab wound. These days, most gore effects have little effect on yours truly—having pretty much seen it all in the last twenty years—but this was just plain icky. God bless the seventies.

Femme fatale Grahame (1922–81)—thoroughly convincing with her Ilsa meets Norman Bates shtick—has a long career of films and television appearances to her credit, spanning thirty seven years from 1944 to 1981, including some the good—David Cronenberg's *The Brood* (1979), the bad—Denis Héroux's *The Uncanny* (1977), and the shoddy—Alfredo Zacharias' *Macabra, La Mano del Diablo* [Macabre, the Hand of the Devil] (1979) aka *Demonoid*. Prolific actor Horst Frank (1929–99) also appeared in such giallos as Dario Argento's *Il Gatto a Nove Code* [The Cat o' Nine Tails] (1971) and Mario Caiano's *L'Occhio nel Labirinto* [The Eye in the Labyrinth] (1972) aka *Blood*. Towards the end of his film career, character actor Carlo de Mejo (1945–) appeared in a slew of Italian splatter films, including some of Lucio Fulci's better known shockers. De Mejo is also the son of Alida Valli (1921–), a once re-spectable actress who later eked out a living with exploitation fare as well.

   L'Etrusco Uccide Ancora was based on a short story by Bryan Edgar Wallace (1904–71), son of prolific mystery writer Edgar Wallace (1875–1932) who, in addition to penning *King Kong* (1933), was almost singlehandedly responsible (posthumously, I might add) for the German krimi film movement of the sixties. Wallace Jr has since been established as a screenwriter for Dario Argento's first three efforts, the far supe-rior giallos *L'Uccello dalle Piume di Cristallo* [The Bird with the Crystal Plumage] (1970), *Il Gatto a Nove Code* and *Quatro Mosche di Velluto Grigio* [Four Flies on Gray Velvet] (1971).

   Director Crispino (1925–) capped a modest ten year career as a filmmaker with the obscure sex comedy *Frankenstein all'Italiana* [Franken-stein Italian style] (1975).

Il Fiume del Grande Caimano (1979)
THE RIVER OF THE GREAT CAIMAN

Dania Film [It] DIR: Sergio Martino PRO: Luciano Martino SCR: Maria Chianetta, Ernesto Gastaldi, Sergio Martino and Luigi Montefiori DOP: Giancarlo Ferrando SFX: Carlo de Marchis and Paolo Ricci MUS: Stelvio Cipriani STR: Rene Abadeza, Barbara Bach, Peter Boom, Claudio Cassinelli, Fabrizia Castagnoli, Silvia Collatina, Clara Colosimo, Giulia d'Angelo, Paul de Odeasie, Lory del Santo, Donald Dias, Christopher Ferrando, Mel Ferrer, Enzo Fisichella, Marco Giannoni, Geneve Hutton, Richard Johnson, Piero Jossa, Marco Mastantuono, Anny Papa, Peter Peiris, Romano Puppo, Bobby Rhodes and D Pauline Skilton

AKA: *Alligators*
   The Big Alligator River
   Der Fluß der Mörderkrokodile [The River of the Killer Crocodile]
   The Great Alligator
   Great Alligator River

Approximately 83m; Color; Rated R
DVD: *The Big Alligator River* [No Shame USA; RTU; WS; NTSC 0] *Der Fluß der Mörderkrokodile* [X-Rated Kult; 85(83)m; WS; PAL R2]
VHS: *The Great Alligator* [Edde Entertainment; 96(83)m; FS; NTSC]
ADL: "Say Goodbye to the Rich and Famous!"

A SMALL STRETCH of African jungle is cleared for Paradise House, a ritzy resort that—in addition to offering wealthy patrons a chance to get away from it all—claims to improve the lo-cal natives' standard of living. Photographer Dan-iel Nessel (Claudio Cassinelli) is hired to capture the tribal customs and the exotic landscape for the resort's travel brochures, and—along with poten-tial love interest Alice Brandt (Barbara Bach), an anthropologist-cum-tour guide—finds himself in a bit of a stew. A couple making like the beast with two backs receive a post coital love bite from an overgrown gecko, a monster the tribespeople believe is the earthly manifestation of their god Cruna. The natives become exceedingly restless and urge the foreigners to leave posthaste, while our heroes encourage the less than receptive di-rector of Paradise House to shut down the fes-tivities, but… well, you know the words.

Mexican lobby card for Il Fiume del Grande Caimano (1979)

Why is it that filmmakers are unable to tell the difference between alligators and crocodiles (or caimans and gavials, for that matter, but let's not split hairs), and use the names of related but different species interchangeably? Probably for the same reason they insist on putting live tarantulas in webs. Easy. They're cheap, and assume horror fans to be too stupid to notice the pathetic cup and ball tactics. Or they are ignorant themselves. Either way, it's irritating, to say the least.

That gripe out of the way, this very Italian Jaws-in-the-tropics sticks to the formula established by Steven Spielberg four years previous, and perpetuated by such memorable entries as Joe Dante's Piranha (1978). Knowing full well it cannot compete with such predecessors, Il Fiume del Grande Caimano tries to up the ante by making the natives an even more formidable threat

than the titular monster, thus playing on the ethnophobic fears already exploited by numerous Green Hell efforts. (Like many of the European cannibal films, Il Fiume del Grande Caimano also makes good use of its exotic locale, a nice change of pace to Spielberg and Dante's more mundane backdrops.)

Performances are for the most part decent (but not exceptional), with contributions from such higher caliber B-names as Mel Ferrer (1917–), Richard Johnson (1927–), and last but not least Barbara Bach (1947–). Bach suffered similar indignities in Sergio Martino's L'Isola degli Uomini Pesce [The Isle of the Fishmen] (1979), which was re-edited with new gore footage and released stateside as Screamers in 1982.

The undisputed star of this film, of course, is the alligator itself. (Or crocodile, or caiman, or

The film does suffer from some jarring, strobe-like edits, and the effects used for the cave-in that marks the film's earth-shattering finale are pretty sad. As far as the makeup effects are concerned, the filmmakers do a passable job of editing between Bloom with an additional head appliance, and the two actors stuffed into the same pair of overalls. Groundbreaking technology it isn't, but one has seen worse. (The same techniques would be improved upon the following year in AIP's next two-headed creature feature, *The Thing with Two Heads*.) Although uncredited, the ape suit was designed (and probably worn) by award winning effects artist Rick Baker, who was just breaking into the business at the time. He would supply the same to AIP's similarly contrived follow up.

Dern's character is supposedly headed for a nervous breakdown, yet his performance is probably the most subdued of his career. In fact, downright lethargic may be a better way to describe his composure. He sees his gardener murdered with a hoe; he blows away a man attempting to rape his wife; and he condemns a retarded man to a hellish ordeal when he decides to graft the killer's head onto his body; but he scarcely blinks or raises his voice throughout. That is, until someone calls him unexpectedly, which sparks an even more unexpected outburst. His sour disposition quickly returns to normal, until later when someone else suggests calling the Sheriff. And so it goes, the only thing getting his goat is Alexander Bell's damnable invention; apparently the doctor suffers from telephone related anxieties to which we, the viewers, are not made privy.

Albert Cole's killer is a leering, cackling psychopath who comes across as a low rent Jon Astin; his scenery chewing certainly accounts for the numerous gaps in his teeth. The film also introduces Bloom, a 7'4" tax accountant who moonlighted in exploitation films playing brain damaged hulks;

US pressbook advertisement for
The Incredible 2-Headed Transplant (1971)
American International Pictures, Inc.

here he kicks off an incredible list of similarly brain damaged productions that includes Al Adamson and Sam Sherman's *Dracula vs Frankenstein* (which also had Cole in a bit part) and *Brain of Blood* (both 1971). Priest—the most popular actress to portray Marilyn, the only normal family member in *The Munsters* (1964–66)—plays Dern's main squeeze; although her hair-don't hasn't changed a lick since the early years, the filmmakers certainly exploit her figure in ways the television show never dared. Even Scooby's sidekick Shaggy—renowned voice actor and disc jockey Casey Kasem—shows up sporting an embarrassing toupee, playing the mad doctor's best friend as well as contributing his talents as a radio announcer.

Director Lanza also made the violent biker flick *The Glory Stompers* (1967).

Although available through the years from various obscure video labels, a beautifully remastered and letterboxed version is available on DVD from MGM's Midnite Movies line of AIP double bills, and is presented completely uncut for the first time (not that we were missing much). Better yet, it shares the disk with Robert Lee Frost's *The Thing with Two Heads*, making this a very welcome double-headed double hitter.

So... where can I get me one of those two-headed bunny rabbits?

It! (1967)

Seven Arts Productions [UK] Goldstar Productions Ltd [US] DIR: Herbert J Leder PRO: Herbert J Leder SCR: Herbert J Leder DOP: Davis Boulton EXP: Robert Goldstein MUS: Carlo Martelli STR: Raymond Adamson, John Baker, Mark Burns, Lindsay Campbell, Tom Chatto, Ernest Clark, Dorothy Frere, Richard Goolden, Brian Haines, Valeria Jill Haworth (aka Jill Haworth), Oliver Johnston, Steve Kirby, Roddy McDowall (aka Roddy MacDowall), Paul Maxwell, Ian McColloch, Russell Napier, Aubrey Richards, Alan Sellers, Frank Sieman and Noel Trevarthen
AKA: *Anger of the Golem*
      Carrasco de Pedra [Executioner of Stone]
      Curse of the Golem
      La Estatua Viviente [The Living Statue]
      Der Golem Lebt! [The Golem Lives]
Approximately 97m; Color; Unrated
ADL: "How can we Destroy it Before it Destroys us?"

ARTHUR PIMM (Roddy McDowall), the assistant curator at a museum, is a proper, likeable chap who has never gotten around to disposing of his mother's corpse, which he keeps around for company. A warehouse used by the museum for storing artifacts burns to the ground; while rooting through the rubble for anything that could be salvaged, Arthur stumbles across a life size stone statue that dates back to the middle of the sixteenth century. The head curator dies a mysterious death, and a very angry Pimm is denied the position due to his young age. Unappeased by his meager £150 annual raise, the already unhinged assistant discovers the secret of the rediscovered Prague golem—a magic scroll bearing the word of God concealed in its hollow toe—and immediately puts this arcane knowledge to good use. Of course, wooing an unobtainable secretary (Jill Haworth) while cutting a swathe to the top takes priority above all else.

Firstly, there is no way I can be truly objective about this film. I remember my first and only exposure to chickenpox; I was six years old, and kept out of school for the better part of a week. One evening, unhindered by a school night's curfew, I stayed up to watch *It!* on the tube, which started at eleven. Within the half hour preceding it, I fell asleep while watching an episode of the controversial but short-lived sitcom *Hot L Baltimore* (1975), and didn't reawaken until the last fifteen minutes of the film, where I was barely conscious enough to appreciate it. This would be the last time any local station would show *It!* for the remainder of the seventies, although I waited those many, many years with baited breath. During the video boom of the eighties, I longed for a sell-through company to give this film a proper release, but no such luck. The nineties proved no more fruitful. Only a few short years ago, I finally acquired a copy from a friend who had recorded it from television; by this time, *It!* had become a childhood grail. So, if my review sounds at all reverential, please do not mistake this for critical admiration. Believe you me, the film has a few problems.

Aside from its nostalgic charm (at least as far as this reviewer is concerned), *It!* has a fair

US lobby card for *It!* (1966) Seven Arts Associated Corporation

amount going for it. The film has the look and feel of some of the later Hammer outings, which isn't much of a surprise when one considers that Seven Arts collaborated with England's reigning horror studio on many illustrious occasions. Although the budget was undoubtedly modest, the film looks sharp throughout.

The film's high points, though, are McDowall and his ruddy co-star. Despite his reservations about the film itself—McDowall never had a kind word to say about *It!*—Roddy turns in a typically ingratiating performance. (As most filmgoers are probably aware, he made his greatest contribution to fantastic cinema when he donned the role of Cornelius in Franklin J Schaffner's 1968 classic *Planet of the Apes*, the character with whom he is still most often identified by geeks like ourselves. McDowall also helmed something of a genre film

in 1971, the somewhat pretentious *The Ballad of Tam Lin*, his sole directorial outing. The film was poorly received in part due to misguided marketing by American International Pictures, which attempted to play up its implied supernatural elements.) Although the character of Arthur Pimm is a delusional megalomaniac, McDowall avoids playing him as a stereotypically raving lunatic, and makes no attempt to mimic Anthony Perkins' twitchiness, even though the character was obviously modeled on Norman Bates. (Presumably as an in joke, one of the players is even named Perkins.)

The golem has a very distinctive mien, which would best be described as a sculpture of Zippy the Pinhead molded from half melted candle wax. Unfortunately, the budget dictated that an actor play the part of the golem even before it is

Mexican lobby card for It! (1966) Seven Arts Associated Corporation

brought to life as a killing machine; it is safe to say that even the most wooden actor would be unable to hold completely still for as long as the scenes demand, thus cluing us in early on that it is nothing more than a person in a papier-mâché costume and not a stone statue awaiting re-animation.

If one considers a conflation of Paul Wegener's *Der Golem* [The Golem] (1920) and Alfred Hitchcock's *Psycho* (1960) as crafty and innovative, then this contrived creature feature is as original as one gets. (Although, if you get right down to it, it's just as much a knock-off of the Universal mummy films, or at least the awful sequels that followed Boris Karloff's chilling contribution.) Thankfully, filmmaker Leder tempers the horror with tongue in cheek humor, but not so much to detract from the vengeance fueled goings-on.

At one point, Mr Pimm is asked, "So that's your new piece?" to which he responds "Yes... that is... *it*." (His emphasis, not mine.) Also, nearing the finale, an old woman who is forced to play host to Pimm and his desiccated mum exclaims, "One more tea with him and his mother will drive me mad!"

Despite some relatively minor lapses of common sense, the story holds up quite well... until the final reel, that is, when all logic is disregarded and the film spirals into pure lunacy. Once Pimm is found to be indirectly responsible for the murders, he holes up in a castle with his lust interest in tow. The military tries to enter the main gate with a single tank, but the shells prove useless against the golem. So, do they try to enter the property from, I don't know, say, another gate while the extremely slow moving golem is distracted or just too far away to pose a threat? No. Do they send in armed paratroopers to rescue the damsel in distress and take out the guy controlling it? No. They simply give up, admit the palace is impregnable, and come to the conclusion that the only solution is to drop a nuclear bomb on the estate. (It's "only a *small* warhead," one of our brain trusts insists.) Honestly, the shifting of gears is so harsh that one might think one had switched channels had the same performers not been involved. I would have fancied the idea that the director died shortly before completing the project, and his imaginative five year old son with his own ideas of how the story should progress stepped in to wrap it up, had Leder not gone on to do another film.

This movie is also cool by its genre associations, in addition to McDowall's contribution. Actress Haworth became something of a B-movie starlet with such films as Michael Armstrong's *Horror House* (1969), Jim O'Connolly's *Tower of Evil* (1972) and Jack Cardiff's *The Mutations* (1973). After working alongside Peter Cushing in Freddie Francis' *The Ghoul* (1974) McCulloch later made a name for himself in many a spaghetti splatter flick, including Lucio Fulci's *Zombi 2* (1979) and Luigi Cozzi's *Contaminazione* [Contamination] (1980).

Filmmaker Leder (1922–83)—who kicked off a sparse but noteworthy career by scripting the creepy and often surreal sci fi horror flick *Fiend Without a Face* (1958)—was also responsible for the so bad it's good cult shocker *The Frozen Dead*, lensed the same year as, and later released on a double bill with, *It!*. A remake of *Fiend Without a Face* is currently under production.

So, just keep telling yourself… *It!* is only a movie… only a movie… only a movie…

Lycanthropus (1961)
LYCANTHROPE

Royal Film Production [Ar/It] DIR: Paolo Heusch (aka Richard Benson) PRO: Guido Giambartolomei (aka Jack Forrest) SCR: Ernesto Gastaldi (aka Julian Berry) DOP: George Patrick MUS: Francis Berman STR: Anne Marie Avis, Lucy Derleth, Herbert Diamonds, Barbara Lass-Kwiatowska (aka Barbara Lass), Curt Lowens, Martha Marker, Maurice Marsac, Mary McNeeran, Patricia Meeker, Joseph Mercer, Grace Neame, Maureen O'Connor, Elizabeth Patrick, Luciano Pigozzi (aka Alan Collins), Carl Schell and Anni Steinert
AKA: *Bei Vollmond Mord* [The Full Moon Murders]
> *The Ghoul in School*
> *Ghoul in a Girls' Dormitory*
> *I Married a Werewolf*
> *Monster Among the Girls*
> *Werewolf in a Girls' Dormitory*
Approximately 83m; b&w; Unrated
DVD: *Werewolf in a Girls' Dormitory* [Alpha Video; 83m; FS; NTSC R1] [Madacy Entertainment; 83m; FS; NTSC R1; Double billed with Blood Creature]
VHS: *Werewolf in a Girls' Dormitory* [Madacy Entertainment; 83m; FS; NTSC R1; Double billed with Blood Creature]
ADL: "Beauties! The Prey of a Monster's Desires!"

TRYING TO LEAVE behind a mysterious accident that left a young woman dead, the young Dr Julian Olcott (Carl Schell) takes up residence as a science professor at a private reformatory for girls; he's no sooner stepped foot on school grounds when the hormonal students begin biting their knuckles over the tutor with the Tab Hunter-like good looks. This particular wolf in the fold is the least of the faculty's worries, for on the night of Olcott's arrival, one of the pupils, Mary, is attacked by a bestial killer when she cuts through the woods surrounding the school after dark. The fact that the underage seductress was on her way back from blackmailing a married

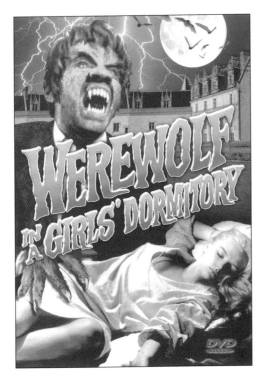

DVD box art for Lycanthropus (2004)
Alpha Video Distributors, Inc. #4465-D

to clear himself of these unfounded accusations, Dr Olcott teams up with Priscilla (Barbara Lass-Kwiatowska), the closest thing to an eyewitness; with the script in need of some forced and maudlin romance, she proves to be no less susceptible to his pheromones than her horny peers.

Lycanthropus is an odd amalgam of old fashioned horror film and sixties giallo style murder mystery; the supernatural/pseudoscientific elements could be completely eliminated without affecting the story in the least, but it is this interesting little contrivance that gives the film an added oomph. Being Euro fare, the storyline is much more complex than it would have been had it been made in the States. It also displays elements that illustrate the growing demand for more risqué, graphic cinema at the time of its release, which of course comes across as fairly innocuous some forty odd years later.

Despite its best efforts, *Lycanthropus* never quite hits the intended target. The film displays camerawork and art direction typical of Italian gothic fare, but the brush strokes of an artist like Bava or Freda are nowhere to be found. The makeup effects on our resident werewolf prove effective when shone in the right light and staged with care, but prove inglorious when the monster strays into the open. (A little less putty and a little more yak hair would have helped considerably, for starters.) The script makes a determined attempt to provide a scientific explanation for lycanthropy, but laying the blame on a faulty pituitary gland proves a little less than satisfactory. (Additionally, many viewers will be annoyed by numerous coincidences, from the hastily discovered antidote, to the fantastic revelation that the teacher's previous brush with the law was the result of a lover who, conveniently enough, was also stricken with intermittent hairy knuckles and a proclivity for walkies by moonlight.)

lover seems to imply that her murder was not a random act of violence.

Suffice to say, everyone becomes a suspect. Was it the unfaithful, skirt chasing teacher with a yen for barely legal teens? Or, more likely, was it his jilted wife? Maybe it was the strict headmistress (Maureen O'Connor), seen stalking the grounds by two students the night of the murder? How about the creepy chauffeur? Or the even sleazier caretaker Walter (Luciano Pigozzi), whose buggy Peter Lorre-like countenance is more than enough to get him slapped with a suspicions charge, regardless of his alibi. Anyone not immune to the dashing newcomer's Aryan charms is laying odds on *him* as the culprit, which seems logical considering the skeletons in his closet, compounded by the fact his appearance precipitated the fiendish murder. Hoping

Top European pressbook advertisement for Lycanthropus (1961) Royal Film Production
Above Theme from Werewolf in a Girls' Dormitory. US single for The Ghoul In School (1961) Cub Records #K-9123

This film stands out in director Heusch's filmography, as he devoted most of his time to action fare. Screenwriter Gastaldi (1934–) has much to his credit, having plied his wares for virtually every Italian filmmaker, from hacks like Umberto Lenzi and Fernando di Leo, to the Big Boot's very own Sergio Leone. He also conspired with exploitation mogul Sergio Martino on many 'illustrious' occasions. (Lurid giallos like *Lo Strano vizio della Signora Wardh* aka *Blade of the Ripper* and *I Corpi Presentano Tracce di Violenza Carnale* aka *Torso*, 1971 and 1973 respectively, come to mind.)

As a bonus, American audiences were treated to *Lycanthropus'* own hip theme song, The Ghoul In School, written by Marilyn Stewart and Frank Owens, performed by The Fortunes with Adam Keefe. For those that care, this Motown inspired tune wouldn't be out of place accompanying a Something Weird Video promotional spot. This little ditty may have a charm all its own, but it does nothing to set the tone for the film to follow. (At least the Wurlitzer laden score that follows the opening credits will keep the closet go-go dancers from slipping on their dancing shoes for the remainder of the film.)

One of the film's biggest benefits is the presence of Barbara Lass-Kwiatowska (1940–95), an alluring young Polish actress who was married to Roman Polanski from 1959 to 1962. Her haunting beauty is not unlike that of Barbara Steele's, and like Ms Steele her talents weren't limited to her comeliness. The rest of the cast performs admirably as well, but she usually demands the viewer's full attention when onscreen. She had my attention, anyway.

MONSTER (1979)

Academy International Distributors [US] DIR: Kenneth Hartford (aka Kenneth Herts) and Herbert L Strock PRO: Kenneth Hartford (aka Kenneth Herts) SCR: Kenneth Hartford (aka Kenneth Herts), Walter Roeber Schmidt, Garland Scott and Herbert L Strock NOV: Monster [Carousel Books; 1979; US PB edition] DOP: Arthur Fitzsimmons and John Wilder Mincey SFX: Steve Czerkas, Kenneth Hartford and Marc Wolf MUS: Gene Kauer STR: Polo C'd Baca, Philip Carey, John Carradine, Monte Cook, Pam Day, Fred Anthony Eisley (aka Tony Eisley), Steven Fisher, Henry Gabaldon, Andrea Hartford, Glen Hartford,

US one-sheet for Monster (1979)
Academy International Distributors

Coral Kassel, John Lamarr, Carolyn Martin, Roberto
Martinez, Jannine May, Leslie Meigs, Jim Mitchum,
Connie Moore, Felicia Robbins, Maria Rubio, Aldo
Sambrell, Emanuel Smith, Luis Suarez and the St
Ann Choir
AKA: *It Came from the Lake*
       Monster, the Legend that Became a Terror
       Monstroid
       The Toxic Horror
       Toxic Monster
Approximately 78m; Color; Rated R
VHS: *It Came from the Lake* [Premiere
Entertainment; 78m; FS; NTSC] Monster
[InterGlobal Video; 85(78)m; FS; NTSC] [Regal
Video; 78m; FS; NTSC] *The Toxic Horror* [Facing
All Death; 78m; FS; NTSC]
ADL: "Buried in the Mud of Countless Centuries,
Something has Begun to Grow…"

"THIS STORY you are about to see is based on
fact. The incident occurred in June 1971 in Co-
lombia." Well, if you believe that, I have a Texas
chain saw massacre I'd like to sell you. Heck, I'll
even throw in a couple of bona fide snuff films if
you act now!

A big rubbery sea monster lurking just off the
shores of a Colombian fishing village makes short
work of unwary lovers straying onto the beach at
night for a quick roll in the sand. One of its intended midnight snacks is a young native woman
who makes the mistake of surviving the ordeal,
claims she was attacked by a demon and is thus
branded as a *bruja* by her superstitious neighbors
(that's "witch" for you gringos in the audience). It
seems the pollutants being pumped into the water by a nearby cement plant—one of the largest
in South America—has taken its toll on the fish-
ermen's livelihood… the very same catch that's
been keeping the behemoth's belly full until now.
An annoying reporter and a pesky revolutionary
do their best to play up the tragedy, but not until Laura—the secretary and on-again, off-again
lover of the plant's owner—is found half eaten on
the beach do the powers that be take action.

What should have been an entertaining low
budget shocker, well, isn't. *Monster's* titular, uhm,
monster takes back seat to the turgid melodrama
that is mired in talking heads and uninteresting
character interplay. (In retrospect, the relentless
sermons on environmentalism and the exploitation of Third World countries with which the
viewers are bludgeoned don't seem so bad.) The
scene of a hand puppet beastie chewing up and
biting in half a bikini clad midnight swimmer
would almost be worth the price of admission,
but the remainder of the film is so gosh darn
mind numbing as to make this little nugget no
better than fool's gold. For most of the film, the
monster doesn't rate more than a few minutes of
screen time. Until the end, that is, when the view-

er gets to see more of its mismatched seams than they probably ever expected or wanted to. (Okay, so he's actually quite lovable with his hinged jaw and Fu Manchu moustache. Scary, no, but lovable, yes.)

"You're crazy if you think I'm going to spend the night out by this *stupid* lake fighting off mosquitoes waiting for you to get a *stupid* picture of a *stupid* monster that'll probably turn out to be a *stupid* log or something," one character complains. And it took no less than *four* screenwriters to dredge up such inspired dialogue? I can't wait to get my hands on the paperback novelization from Carousel Books mentioned in the closing credits, if indeed it ever was published. (I've been looking, but—alas—no such luck.)

Technically, the film is only a notch, maybe two, better than someone's 8mm home movies. Of course, much of the footage looks like a vacation travelogue, so this may not be that far off the mark. Most of the above sea level footage was actually shot in South America, successfully capturing the local flavor; most of the underwater sequences, on the other hand, were filmed on location in someone's swimming pool.

Some of the performers who made the mistake of wandering onto this particular set include James Mitchum (eldest son of Mr *Cape Fear* himself, Robert); Tony Eisley (whose long history of genre films includes having worked for Al Adamson, Ted V Mikels, Oliver Drake, and David L Hewitt—the latter of whom functioned as the mechanical effects artist on *Monster* as well); and a frail looking John Carradine (whose contributions to the genre are even more exhaustive than Eisley's). One may be inclined to ask, "Why the long face, John?" (sorry... I just couldn't resist) but I doubt any self respecting thespian would be pleased if they were forced to eke out a living in their golden years by slumming in movies like this. (Apparently, John confided to one of the

VHS box art for Monster (1988)
Facing All Death Video #FAD-2

film's crew members on the set of *Monster*, "This is the *worst* piece of shit I've ever worked on... and I've worked on a *lot* of pieces of shit.")

Director Hartford (aka Herts) helmed a handful of other exploitation films, as well as producing Herbert Strock's *The Devil's Messenger* (1962) starring Lon Chaney Jr, and scripting Mohy Quandour's obscure shocker *The Spectre of Edgar Allan Poe* (1964). Co-conspirator Strock (1918–) returned to the horror genre after a conspicuous sixteen year absence. One can't help but wonder why he would risk tarnishing a reputation that included *Blood of Dracula* (1957), *I Was* a *Teenage Frankenstein* (1957) and *The Crawling Hand* (1963) with this turkey.

As of this writing, the Internet Movie Database (IMDb) also lists the presence of actors Stella Calle, Roger Clark, Fernando Corredor, Jack Lamont, Diane McBain, Glen Ransom, Kelly Sill and Jade Stuart, yet fails to include all but three of the cast members actually listed in the screen credits. To make matters more confusing, several video boxes insist character actor Keenan Wynn is a participant, even though he had the smarts to just say no.

I know that it probably doesn't deserve it, but this film is in desperate need of restoration and re-mastering, as all the available prints (most being from sell-through public domain video outfits) are jumpy, grainy, blurry, scratchy, underexposed, and generally unwatchable. Fitting, I know.

Ultimately, *Monster* lacks the charm of such waterlogged peers as *The Crater Lake Monster* (1977) and fares no better than Amando de Ossorio Rodríguez's sad, sad swansong *Serpiente de Mar* [The Sea Serpent] (1984).

IL MOSTRO DI VENEZIA (1965)
THE MONSTER OF VENICE

IGondola Film [It] Walter Manley Enterprises [US] DIR: Dino Tavella PRO: Walter Manley and Christian Marvel SCR: Paolo Lombardo, Gian Battista Mussetto, Dino Tavella and Antonio Walter DOP: Mario Parapetti EXP: Walter Manley and Christian Marvel MUS: Marcello Gigante STR: Francesco Bagarrini, Alba Brotto, Maureen Lidgard Brown, Elmo Caruso, Roberto Contero, Viki del Castillo, Gaetano dell'Era, Luciano Gasper, Alcide Gazzotto, Antonio Grossi, Jack Judd, Luigi Martocci (aka Gin Mart), Carlo Russo, Anita Todesco, Paolo Vaccari, Maria Rosa Vizzina and Pietro Walter AKA: *The Embalmer*
　　　Het Monster van Venetie [The Monster of Venice]
　　　Le Monstre de Venise [The Monster of Venice]
Approximately 83m; b&w; Unrated
DVD: *The Embalmer* [Alpha Video; 79(77)m; WS; NTSC R1] VHS: The Embalmer [Something Weird Video; 77m; FS; NTSC]
ADL: "Beauty After Beauty Dragged to a Sunken Crypt… Petrified Play Captives of the Embalmer"

BY DAY, a cowled, skull faced killer ambles about his subterranean abode beneath the streets of Venice—that's Italy, to be precise, not California—pausing only to admire his bevy of preserved female corpses. By night, he dons a wetsuit and scuba gear and lurks the canals, waiting to jump out and abduct any unwary female prey that strays too close to the water's edge. Our resident sociopath has a penchant for eighteen year old girls, and—as luck would have it—a busload of barely legal students from Rome arrives, improving his odds dramatically. (Especially since he usually hangs out in the basement of the hotel in which they're all conveniently registered. Who would've thunk it?)

Looking into the murders is Andreas, a reporter who "looks as slick as a movie idol" (which, he insists, can be achieved with nothing more than a good razor at one's disposal). He is convinced that "Venice is hiding a monster!" and that a "maniacal sex fiend" is responsible, despite the fact that the bodies of the missing teenagers—all presumed drowned—have yet to surface, and thus no evidence of murder, much less sexual misconduct. (A very unsure police inspector can't discount his theories, sticking to his guns that, "Maybe, I don't know, *probably* that's the story.") Short on evidence, Andreas decides to take some time out of his busy hypothesizing to play tour guide to the gaggle of schoolgirls in order to make time with their chaperone (Maureen Lidgard Brown).

Here's the equation, for those who feel the need to bone up on their cinematic arithmetic:

Phantom of the Opera – the opera + a wetsuit and scuba gear + (object of obsession x however many young women the budget could afford) + implied necrophilia + trophy fetishism – good taste – common sense = *Il Mostro di Venezia*. Throw in a liberal dash of tedium, leave the whole mess to sit half baked for approximately ninety minutes, and you have a kitchen recipe as well as a mathematical formula.

Il Mostro di Venezia is not the most unpalatable Eurotrash burger one might find oneself taking a bite out of, but only those with a cast iron gut will be spared the imminent heartburn that follows. Although very reminiscent of the poverty row horrors of the forties inspired by the likes of pulp mystery writer Edgar Wallace, there may be enough sixties staples to keep things interesting for those who think b&w film is a bad thing (there's even some peeping tom action to sleazen things up a bit). The film is slow early on, and the maniac's exploits seem almost secondary to the snooze inducing drama, but the last reel boasts some nice atmosphere and at least one unexpected plot development that seems a little chancy for the time… compared to what we've come to expect from modern Hollywood cinema, anyway, if you discount the likes of *Se7en* (1995).

The film is a mixed bag throughout. Given, the story is wonderfully contrived, but the execution is often pedestrian, with the filmmakers fumbling behind the camera hoping they've got enough usable footage to make a feature length film. (Even the performers take their own sweet time, hoping to drag this sucker out to the prerequisite ninety minutes. They fail in their attempts, as does the editor who was probably none too pleased that there wasn't enough stock to make it a coherent eighty, even with his incessant recycling.) Either the outside scenes were shot in the dead of winter, or the cinematographer was suffering from low blood sugar during these ex-

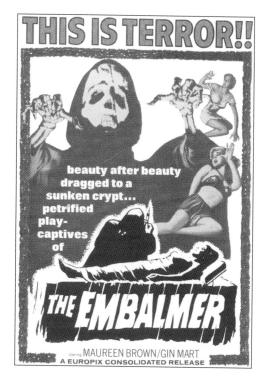

US pressbook advertisement for
Il Mostro di Venezia (1966) Europix Consolidated

cursions, if the jittery camerawork is any indication. The pounding score is far too Wagnerian to be effective, especially when it assaults the nearly deafened viewer during the stalking and abduction scenes, doing nothing to elicit tension. Of course, the filmmakers have done everything in their power to dispense with suspense altogether from the get-go, even going so far as to disclosing the identity of the forthcoming victim with an unnecessary freeze frame on them and their regrettable hair-don'ts. Or straining the viewer's suspension of disbelief by having the killer sneak up on an unsuspecting victim in the woods in the dead of night while wearing flippers. (I guess they couldn't hear the sounds of his approach, with the pounding score drowning it out and all.)

With lines like "My secret potion will penetrate every cell in your body!," or "To ascertain the

How about: "I've heard of stereophonic sound, but this is ridiculous!"
US promotional gag card teaser for Il Mostro di Venezia (1966) Europix Consolidated

facts I've gathered I'll have to review my findings," the English voiceovers are guaranteed to tickle the unintentional funny bone of most *Trashfiend* readers. And if by chance the viewer actually laments such horrible dubbing, their opinion of the superiority of original language prints may be challenged by a musical number performed by a grating rock'n'roll troubadour who is allowed to wail in his native tongue.

Then there is our villainous Venetian who chews the scenery in the privacy of his underground hidey hole, describing his every intent and every action to the embalmed beauties, actresses trying desperately not to breathe or flinch as they stand in their cubicles wrapped only in a sheet. Presumably, his monologues are intended to keep the viewer abreast of the obvious… although its effect is to ultimately lull the unwitting spectator into a stupor. But, hey, he looks like he was modeled on the Crimson Ghost from *Cyclotrode X* (1946), so he gets points for *looking* cool even if he is a pompous, longwinded git.

The most unnerving aspect of this film is that, apparently, the killer wears his wetsuit under his clothes much of the time, which I would assume makes for very uncomfortable underwear. (The authorities would have no difficulty tracking him down, if they would just think to follow the damnable squeaking.) Hands down, the film's most frightening, utterly nerve wracking moment is when a frail elderly woman, looking as if she just stepped out of a Nazi concentration camp, decides to get funky on the dance floor with a club orchestra. I'm sure the question "Will she suffer an aneurysm—or at the very least throw out her hip—before the number is finished?," is on every last viewer's mind, and that the tension this scene creates is universally palpable. The second most horrifying scene involves a man being cheerfully swarmed by a horde of pigeons; luckily, we are spared the sight of the inevitable whitewashing.

Avella (1920–69) made only one other film, the forgotten war flick *Una Sporca Guerra* [One Dirty War] (1964). Most of the other people

Belgian window card for
Il Mostro di Venezia (1965) Cosmopolis Films

THE NIGHT CALLER (1965)

Armitage Films Ltd [UK] New Art Productions Inc. [UK] DIR: John Gilling PRO: Ronald Liles and John J Phillips SCR: Jim O'Connolly NOV: The Night Callers by Frank Crisp [John Long; 1960; UK HC edition] The Night Callers by Frank Crisp [Panther Books; 1963; UK PB edition] DOP: Stephen Dade EXP: John Phillips MUS: Johnny Gregory STR: Ballard Berkeley, Alfred Burke, John Carson, Robert Crewdson, Maurice Denham, Barbara French, Tom Gill, Romo Gorrara, David Gregory, Patricia Haines, Vincent Harding, Douglas Livingstone, Geoffrey Lumsden, Stanley Meadows, Warren Mitchell, Aubrey Morris, John Saxon, John Sherlock, Marianne Stone, Anthony Wager and Jack Watson
AKA: *Blood Beast from Outer Space*
The Night Caller from Outer Space
Approximately 84m; b&w; Unrated
DVD: *The Night Caller from Outer Space* [Image Entertainment; 84m; WS; NTSC R1]
VHS: *The Night Caller from Outer Space* [Image Entertainment; 84m; WS; NTSC]
ADL: "Space Creatures Snatch Girls to Mysterious Planet"

involved with *Il Mostro di Venezia* had similarly abbreviated careers, save for Anita Todesco, who appeared in a slew of non genre efforts, mostly action films. Co-producer Manley (1918–96) was at least partly to blame for the slew of low budget futura nouveau imports that deluged drive ins during the sixties; given that *The Green Slime* was one of them, we'll forgive him such transgressions.

Originally released in the US alongside Michael Reeves' *La Sorella di Satana* (1966) aka *The She-Beast*, this film was later re-issued as the bottom rung of a horror marathon triple bill below Ted V Mikels' *The Corpse Grinders* (1971) and the HG Lewis inspired gore-omedy *The Undertaker and his Pals* (1967) before fading into obscurity for almost thirty years.

TWO SCIENTISTS, Dr Morley (Maurice Denham) and his protégée Jack Costain (John Saxon), rush after a meteorite that displays enigmatic qualities, only to find that the military is already combing the English countryside for it. Expecting to find something rather enormous, they instead discover that the source of the commotion is a soccer sized rock seemingly piloted to Earth via remote control. They waste no time in hauling it to Falsley Park—a government run radio and electronic research facility—for a battery of tests, and discover it to be a hollow sphere composed of selenium and housing a vacuum. Whereas the brass is convinced that they have appropriated a rogue Commie satellite, the eggheads are more than a little certain that it is instead extraterrestrial in origin. After the scientist's secretary is accosted in the office after

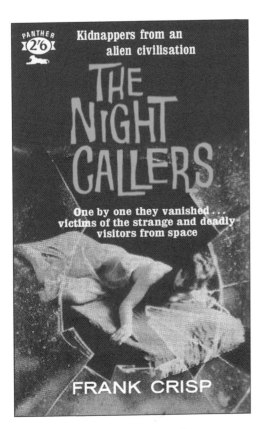

Kidnappers from an alien civilisation

PANTHER 2'6

THE Night CALLERS

One by one they vanished...
victims of the strange and deadly
visitors from space

FRANK CRISP

UK paperback novelization for
The Night Caller (1963) Panther Books

hours by a clawed man-like creature that inexplicably appears in the sealed storage room in which the sphere has been sequestered, the white coats come to the conclusion that it is actually a matter transreceiver, capable of teleporting its creators to Earth from Jupiter's moon, Ganymede.

One such bug-eyed monster makes the jump a second time, then fights its way off the base. Having successfully carjacked its own set of wheels, the uninvited guest then proceeds to lure and ultimately abduct local birds through a wanted advert in *Bikini Girl* magazine, its intentions unknown but probably not in the least honorable. (With twenty one girls spirited away in less than three weeks, one has to assume he's stocking up for the long haul.)

Without a doubt, *The Night Caller*'s greatest strength lies in its sharp scriptwriting. First, most of the film is populated by realistic and/ or interestingly offbeat characters; whereas the leads usually fall into the first category; others— like the sleazy owner of a used bookstore who is unknowingly in cahoots with the spooky space invader—would not be out of place in an early Argento film. To augment the characters is some unexpected but very welcome dry humor; a scene with the Major (John Carson) trying futilely to explain the research team's scientific findings to his superior over the phone is uproarious, and another with authorities interviewing the distraught parents of a missing girl is also not without its chuckles. Second, *The Night Caller* offers a fairly realistic portrayal of science and its inner workings. Even when the details are flawed or the concepts farfetched, the scientists act like scientists and their explanations sound plausible. Of course, none of this would have meant a damn if the performers had not been up to the task, and it should surprise no one that the movie was based—fairly faithfully, by most accounts—on a novel by Frank Crisp, a prolific British writer who specialized in sea adventures.

The film also plays against formulaic types, especially in the casting of a somewhat manly secretarial love interest, and a dour faced superintendent working the case. The Major who works as the go-between for the military and the scientific researchers also avoids the clichés that usually accompany such a character. Throw in an unexpected dissolution for one of the major players, topped off with a rather downbeat finale, and you have a film that proves engaging throughout because it avoids the paint by numbers trappings.

The realization of the film is fairly straightforward, proving itself competent while avoiding any artistic flourishes. The special effects are modest (typical of English sci fi fare at the time), which in

chair bound woman in a locked cage, her ride parked just outside, and coming to the conclusion that it *must* have been an accident. This is after they discover the groundskeeper dead, having been bitten by a venomous snake and then buried alive. I guess this is to counterbalance the many films in which suspicions are aroused without the slightest shred of evidence or motive.

Being early seventies Eurotrash, the film is not without its gratuity, which is part of the reason *La Notte Che Evelyn Uscì dalla Tomba* is so gosh darn watchable. Damn near every woman who wanders onto the set doffs her clothes at some point. (Unfortunately, even the longest print available—which clocks in at roughly ninety eight minutes—is shorn of some of the skin.) Most of the violence is rather tame, save for a scene where one victim's body is dragged into a cage of starved foxes and promptly stripped and eviscerated, confirming that the effects budget was not so destitute they couldn't afford a bucket of pig gut. One of the murders, though, which has one nosey victim being beaten to death with a rock, is unintentionally comic, thanks to her reaction to the attack and the inappropriate sound effects that accompany the bludgeoning.

Suspense is kept to a bare minimum, and the shocks are practically nonexistent; the scene in which the titular wraith is finally seen to actually rise from her tomb probably wouldn't leave an impression on anyone over the age of seven. The only facet of the film that could truly be considered nightmarish is that it features a cadre of maids in service to the playboy who—because of his pathological hair fetish—are forced to wear Little Orphan Annie wigs when on duty. Trust me, you'll shudder too at the sight.

After being featured in a godforsaken number of spaghetti westerns, de Teffè (1932–) broadened his exploitation horizons and appeared in such genre efforts as the Barbara Steele vehi-

cle *Un Angelo per Satana* [An Angel for Satan] (1966), *Sette Scialli di Seta Gialla* [Seven Shawls of Yellow Silk] (1972) and *Femmine Infernali* [Women's Inferno] (1979). Enrica Bianchi Colombatto (1942–) is still keeping busy as an actress, and has such memorable trash horror films to her credit as *La Plus Longue Nuit du Diable* [The Longest Night of the Devil] (1971) aka *The Devil's Nightmare*, *Hexen Geschändet und zu Tode Gequält* [Witches Raped and Tortured to Death] (1972) aka *Mark of the Devil, Part II* and the Paul Naschy vehicle *Una Libéluna para Cada Muerto* [A Dragonfly for Each Corpse] (1974). Memorable by my standards, anyway.

Director Miraglia (1924–) made only a handful of films between 1967 and 1972, his swansong being *La Dama Rossa Uccide Sette Volte* [The Red Queen Kills Seven Times] (1972), a giallo notable for featuring a young Sybil Danning.

When it comes down to it, *La Notte Che Evelyn Uscì dalla Tomba* is a guilty pleasure that, from all reports, many others feel guilt-ridden for liking as well.

IL PLENILUNIO DELLE VIRGINI (1973)
THE FULL MOON OF THE VIRGINS

Virginia Cinemtografica [It] DIR: Luigi Batzella (aka Paolo Solvay, aka Paul Solvay) SCR: Alan M Harris and Massimo Pupillo (aka Ralph Zucker) DOP: Aristide Massaccesi (aka Michael Holloway) EXP: Massimo Pupillo (aka Ralph Zucker) MUS: Vasili Kojucharov STR: Esmerelda Barros, Mark Damon, Girogio Dolfin (aka George Dolfin), Gengher Gatti (aka Alexander Getty), Rosalba Neri (aka Sara Bay), Stefano Oppedisano (aka Stephen Hopper), Xiro Papas (aka Ciro Papas), Sergio Pislar and Enza Sbordone (aka Francesca Romana Davila) AKA: *The Devil's Wedding Night*
 De Maagden van de Volle Maan [The Virgins of the Full Moon]

VHS box art for Il Plenilunio delle Virgini
(circa 1984) Wizard Video #038

Pleine Lune [Full Moon]
Vierges de la Pleine Lune [Virgins of the Full
Moon]
Les Vierges Maudites De Dracula [The
Cursed Virgins of Dracula]
Approximately 84m; Color; Rated R
VHS: *The Devil's Wedding Night* [VCI; 85(84)m;
FS; NTSC] [Wizard Video; 85(84)m; FS; NTSC]
Pleine Lune [Dynasty Films; RTU; FS; SECAM]
Les Vierges Maudites De Dracula [Space Video;
RTU; FS; SECAM]
ADL: "Dark Desires Unleash the Legions of
Lucifer!"

KARL SCHILLER (Mark Damon), a young archeologist, discovers proof of the existence of the mythical Ring of the Nibelungen, whose stone was extricated from an ancient meteorite in the Carpathian Mountains. ("When moonlight strikes its surface, weird, eerie and uncanny phenomenon takes place," his source insists.) He tracks down its current whereabouts to Transylvania ("vampire country"), but before he can be on his way, his libertine twin Franz borrows his studious brother's magical amulet and heads east to search out the ring on his lonesome. After seducing the innkeeper's daughter, Franz makes his way to Castle Dracula, having left his only safeguard at the local watering hole. Only a day behind his opportunistic sibling, Karl arrives at the castle just in time for the 'Night of the Virgin Moon,' an event that takes place every fifty years where five village virgins are beckoned to the crumbling stronghold, never to be heard from again.

Il Plenilunio delle Virgini is another ham fisted stab at sexing up Bram Stoker's popular formula, but—being low rent gothicism wallowing in the excesses of seventies trash horror—it cannot compare to even the worst of Hammer's Dracula inspired period pieces. The staples are present and accounted for: an old castle backdrop, creaking doors, glue-on mutton chops, and—last but not least—vampyros lesbos, seventies style. And, yes, there's even the occasional sound of a fuzzed out guitar thrown in to distract the viewer from a horde of anachronisms fostered by the obvious budgetary constraints. The opening credits set the stage for this Eurotrash offering, proffering scenes of an all-female orgy spliced with its participants having their throats slit as seen through a blood red filter, but, alas, the film is rarely able to live up to such promising foreplay. *Il Plenilunio delle Virgini* displays more breasts than bite, as this opening scene is far more gratuitous than anything found in the remaining eighty plus minutes.

The gore consists of some gushing stab wounds, a handful of dry decaps, and a bloody dismemberment, but these are all saved for the end of the last reel… far too late to rouse the unwary viewers from their necessitated slumber.

What separates this film from its peers are not its good points, but its faults and occasional chutzpah. An otherwise tedious and uneventful sex scene has the woman transforming into a giant bat mid coitus. Our hero is later accosted by a bald, hunchbacked vampire whose enormous fangs are only eclipsed by his shaggy eyebrows. The stone in Countess Dracula's ring—as ungainly and gaudy as one might expect from such a dime store deus ex machina—looks suspiciously like a partially flattened cherry tomato in a cracker jack fitting. The viewers' sympathies are not directed towards the unwilling maidens, or the valiant heroes, but the poor horses that have apparently galloped at full speed from London to the Carpathian Mountains without so much as a breather. Furthermore, references to Edgar Allan Poe and Richard Wagner's operas are conflicting, and the devil god Pazuzu is referred to by a scholar as Egyptian, not Abyssinian or Babylonian as anyone with a basic grasp of mythology or the occult would have known, even in the mid 1800s. (Of course, modern filmgoers know this because of *The Exorcist*, but that's neither here nor there.) Unfortunately, even reveling in the film's so bad it's good qualities do nothing to make the film any less yawn inspiring.

Director Luigi Batzella was also responsible for such gratuitous shockers as *Nuda per Satana* [Nude for Satan] (1974) and the Nazi camp grungefest *La Bestia in Calore* [The Beast in Heat] (1977) aka *SS Hell Camp*. Scriptwriter Massimo Pupillo (1929–82) made his own contributions as a genre director with the similarly lurid (but more professionally made) *Il Boia Scarlatto* [The Scarlet Hangman] (1965) aka *Bloody Pit of Horror* and *5 Tombe per un Medium* [Five Tombs for a Medium] (1966) aka *Terror-Creatures from the Grave*. And of course, cinematographer Aristide Massaccesi (1936–99), the only person to employ almost as many pseudonyms as the infamous Jesse Franco, later went on to direct far more interesting exploitation horror films, such as *Buio Omega* [Blue Holocaust] (1979) aka *Buried Alive* and *Anthropophagous the Beast* [Man-Eater] (1980) aka *The Grim Reaper*.

According to the American pressbook distributed by Dimension Pictures, the theatrical release of this film boasted a recitation of Edgar Allan Poe's poem Annabel Lee as performed by Vincent Price, but apparently it was removed for the later video releases. A possible copyright infringement? Who knows.

SEDDOK, L'EREDE DI SATANA (1960)
SEDDOK, THE HEIR OF SATAN

Leone Film [Fr/It] DIR: Mario Bava (aka Mario Fava) and Anton Giulio Majano (aka Richard McNamara) PRO: Mario Bava (aka Mario Fava) SCR: Alberto Bevilacqua, Gino de Santis, Anton Giulio Majano and Piero Monviso DOP: Aldo Giordani SFX: Ugo Amadoro MUS: Armando Trovajoli STR: Roberto Bertea, Sergio Fantoni, Rina Franchetti, Ivo Garrani, Susanne Loret, Alberto Lupo, Glamor Mora, Franca Parisi, Giovanna Piaz (aka Gianna Piaz) and Andrea Scotti
AKA: *Atom Age Vampire*
  Le Monstre au Masque [The Monster with a Mask]
  Seddok der Würger mit den Teufelskrallen [Seddok the Strangler with the Devil Claws]
  Seddok, El Heredero del Diablo [Seddok, the Heir of the Devil]
  Seddok, Son of Satan
Approximately 105m; b&w; Unrated

...BEFORE YOUR VERY EYES THE TERRIFYING TRANSFORMATION OF MAN INTO MONSTER!

ATOM AGE VAMPiRE

SUSANNE LORET
ALBERT LUPO
A TOPAZ FILM CORP. RELEASE

US lobby card for Seddok, l'Erede di Satana (1963) Topaz Film Corporation

DVD: *Atom Age Vampire* [Alpha Video; 87(69)m; FS; NTSC R1] [Madacy Entertainment; 87m; FS; NTSC R1; Double feature with *Bloodlust*]

VHS: *Atom Age Vampire* [Acme Video; 87m; FS; NTSC] [Madacy Entertainment; 87m; FS; NTSC; Double feature with *Bloodlust*] [Rhino Video; 87m; FS; NTSC]

ADL: "Before Your Very Eyes the Terrifying Transformation of Man into Monster!"

MISS JEANETTE MORENEAU (Susanne Loret) is dumped by her main squeeze because she won't give up her job as an actress (or stripper, I'm not sure which. Things can get hazy in the poor translations of non English speaking imports). Distraught, she does a nosedive off a cliff in her convertible and survives, albeit "horribly" scarred. Although her disfigurement looks as if it could be easily remedied by some rudimentary plastic surgery, she is pronounced a hopeless case by the medical community at large and left to wallow in her malaise, hiding her scars with a peek-a-boo hairdo à la Veronica Lake. A scientist, Professor Alberto Levin (Alberto Lupo), offers his services, looking for a guinea pig on which to test Derma-28, a "miraculous therapy" that uses radiation to stimulate new tissue growth. During the treatment, he becomes obsessed with the retired performer, going so far as to knock off his jealous female assistant, Monique (Franca Parisi).

He cures his newfound love interest, but the process soon reverses itself; in order to test it more thoroughly, he injects himself and—in true Jekyll & Hyde fashion—turns into a crusty faced beastie who begins roaming the streets, attacking women and stealing the glands needed to perfect his formula. (Only by immersing himself in irradiated gas can he return to his former self.) In a reversal of Poe's 'The Murders in the Rue Morgue,' an escaped gorilla is blamed for the murders. (Why an ape would remove its victims' glands with a scalpel is anyone's guess.)

I haven't seen the original European version of this film (which runs almost twenty minutes longer than the American cut), but I have a gut feeling the English language print has been heavily rewritten and re-edited to compensate for the missing footage. (The fact it also lists an American director who was not originally involved in the project may have clued me in as well.) Aside from the addition of the Robert Louis Stevenson styled antics, *Seddok, l'Erede di Satana* is standard post *Les Yeux sans Visage* fare. Lacking the flair of Georges Franju's 1959 classic, this knock-off replaces poetry with prurience, filling the gaps with inexplicable monster transformations and titillating panty shots.

Scenery chewing abounds, exaggerated by the poor dubbing. The first reel plays like an infomercial for the nonexistent Derma-28, steeped in pseudoscientific claptrap that could only be conceived by a hack comic book writer. The lumpy makeup prosthetics sported by our resident mad scientist are reminiscent of those worn by his peer in the pleasantly hackneyed *Monster on the Campus* (1958). During his first transformation, the filmmakers opted for awkward stop motion photography to facilitate the change, but reverted to the standard dissolve metamorphosis later on.

Screenwriter Bevilacqua (1934–) later worked with Bava on two of his more 'colorful' efforts, *I Tre Volti della Paura* [The Three Faces of Fear] (1963) aka *Black Sabbath*, and *Terrore nello Spazio* [Terror in Space] (1965) aka *Planet of the Vampires*. His final contribution to the genre was narrating the shockumentary *Angeli Bianchi... Angeli*

French pressbook advertisement for *Seddok, l'Erede di Satana* (1960) Leone Film

Neri [White Angel... Black Angel] (1970) aka *Witchcraft '70*, which boasts a rare screen appearance by Anton LaVey, founder of the Church of Satan. Bevilacqua later became a noted novelist, translating his own books to the screen.

This was the only horror film helmed by prolific director/screenwriter Majano (1909–94) although he was responsible for the English dubbing on *Il Mulino delle Donne di Pietra* [The Mill of the Stone Women] (1960). Bava was only credited as producer, but actually functioned as a co-director on this film as well. We can probably assume he was responsible for the few interestingly staged scenes, but even then his contributions seem moot. Hindered by its insistence on playing everything by the book, *Seddok, l'Erede di Satana* amounts to little more than dime store monster fare. Unfortunately for most trashfiends, the film offers surprisingly little in the way of so bad it's good entertainment.

Mexican lobby card for Seddok, l'Erede di Satana (1963) Columbia Pictures

El Sonido Prehistórico (1964)
THE PREHISTORIC SOUND

Zurbano Films, S.A. [Spain] DIR: Jose Antonio
Nieves Conde PRO: Gregorio Sacristán de Hoyas
(aka Gregorio Sacristan) SCR: Sam X Abarbanel,
Jose Antonio Nieves Conde, Gregorio Sacristán de
Hoyas (aka Gregorio Sacristan) and Gregg Tallas
DOP: Manuel Berenguer SFX: Manuel Baquero
MUS: Luis de Pablo STR: José Bódalo, Antonio
Casas, Arturo Fernández, Lola Gaos, Soledad
Miranda, James Philbrook, Francisco Piquer and
Ingrid Pitt
AKA: *Prigionieri dell'Orrore* [Prisoners of Horror]
       El Sonido de la Muerte [The Sound of Death]
       Sound of Horror
Approximately 91m; b&w; Unrated
DVD: *Sound of Horror* [Alpha Video; 90m; FS;
NTSC R1]

A SMALL GROUP of war veterans who acquired pieces of a map giving the location of Gre-
cian artifacts stolen during WWII band together
in order to share the wealth; while looking for
their booty in a cave avoided by the superstitious
locals, they inadvertently unearth the mummi-
fied remains of a beautifully preserved Neander-
thal and a nest of petrified eggs. One of the latter
hatches into an invisible blob like creature that
wastes little time in brunching on an impatient
treasure hunter, who is later found mauled to
death and completely drained of blood. It's thirst
unquenched, the prehistoric monstrosity chases
the lot of them to an isolated house in which they
are staying, its presence given away only by its
screams. (Well, that, and the low budget havoc it
leaves in its frenzied wake.)

This movie exploits one of my favorite ideas conceived by frugal horror filmmakers: if you can't afford the special effects that come with having a monster as the star, simply make it invisible! *Orloff y el Hombre Invisible* [Orloff and the Invisible Man] (1970) dispensed with most of the film's special effects budget by employing this oh-so-clever legerdemain, as have others on occasion. Surprisingly, this cheat as it is applied to *El Sonido Prehistórico* actually contributes to the suspense, and benefits it in other areas by taking the sober less is more credo of older horror movies to an almost ludicrous extreme. (The importance of the latter becomes apparent when we finally get to see the bargain basement beastie in silhouette, as it looks like something that could be found in a lesser *kaijû eiga* effort.) Of course, there is never an explanation as to *why* our resident carnivore is invisible to the naked eye.

El Sonido Prehistórico is one of the few monster movies to be produced in Spain prior to their horror 'renaissance,' kick started three years later with the first entry in Paul Naschy's werewolf cycle *La Marca del Hombre Lobo* [The Mark of the Wolfman] (1968) and Amando de Ossorio Rodríguez's tongue in cheek *Malenka, la Sobrina del Vampiro* [Malenka, the Niece of the Vampire] (1968). (The prolific Jesús Franco Manera had already paved the way for Spanish horror in general with *Gritos en la Noche* [Cries in the Night] in 1962, but this *Les Yeux sans Visage* inspired shocker focused on gory surgery footage, not stock monsters, which was curiously more acceptable by the censors.)

The direction of *El Sonido Prehistórico* is often pedestrian, recalling the lower end horror fare being produced in Mexico at the time. The film takes its time getting to the heart of the matter—the first thirty minutes are laboriously talky, even for those of us who like a little story and characterization to accompany the mayhem—and there are a few too many lulls between the first 'appear-

Spanish one-sheet art for
El Sonido Prehistórico (1964) ARCE Films

ance' of the monster and the anticlimactic finale (which is made worse by the false ending at the seventy minute mark).

What this film *does* have going for it is a reasonably sound script: aside from the contrived nature of the prehistoric antagonist, the scriptwriters' clever reworking of familiar materials is refreshing, and holds up well in light of the now dated formula. Several conventions that the viewer may expect are carefully avoided, including the clichés of greed intensely explored by John Huston in *Treasure of the Sierra Madre* (1948) then clumsily swiped by countless screenwriters thereafter. (When it comes to dying a violent death or being poor but very much alive, most of our cast decides that being on the dole isn't so bad a prospect, and thus try to pull out while the going's still

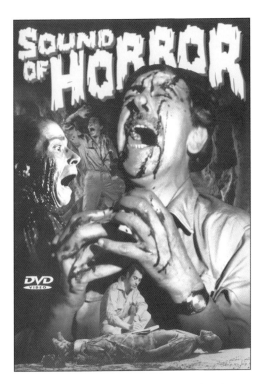

DVD box art for El Sonido Prehistórico (2003)
Alpha Video Distributors, Inc. #4191-D

good.) *El Sonido Prehistórico* also boasts the type of claustrophobia best represented by George A Romero's *Night of the Living Dead* (1968); much like the seminal modern zombie flick, the house itself becomes a character in the tense proceedings. In fact, most of the script's shortcomings correlate with the monster itself. Our feature creature has no problem smashing through reinforced doors, yet the house's flimsy shutters manage to keep it at bay. Additionally, a couple of thrown axes give it far more grief than several crates of dynamite detonated in its lap. (There is also the matter of rampant sexism, but this is typical of Eurotrash of the sixties and seventies, so it will be reluctantly forgiven.)

On display in *El Sonido Prehistórico* are some fairly grisly deaths, mostly presented as after-the-fact gore. The cave settings—if they are in fact

man made—are quite convincing and contribute to the film's atmosphere. Overall, the special effects and art direction is commendable. Again, only those aspects related to the monster—like the 'sound of horror' which makes one just want to bitch slap the creature, and the unsatisfying visual effects punctuating the finale—are disappointing.

El Sonido Prehistórico was early in the careers of its two female stars, namely Soledad Miranda and Ingrid Pitt. Miranda (1943–70) had secured a career in genre films working for Spanish auteur Jesús Franco Manera in the few short years before her untimely death in an automobile accident, appearing in such erotic horror films as *Les Cauchemars Naissent la Nuit* [Nightmares are Born at Night] (1970) and *Las Vampiras* [The Vampire's Women] (1971). This was the screen debut of Pitt (1937–); although her contributions to the horror genre are few and far between, the image of the actress baring her bloodied fangs and ample bosom in one of several promotional stills taken from *The House that Dripped Blood* (1970) has secured her a place in the hearts of all horror fans that have ever had even a passing erotic thought about female vampires.

In a film career that spanned thirty eight years as a writer and director, this was the only horror outing for Conde (1915–). Co-scriptwriter Tallas had a handful of films to his directorial credit, including the dreary but almost engaging shocker *The Nightmare Never Ends* (1980), which was later truncated and worked into the inexcusable horror anthology *Night Train to Terror* (1985).

When it was originally released stateside, *El Sonido Prehistórico* was shown as part of a double bill that also included Mario Bava's *Operazione Paura* aka *Kill, Baby, Kill!* Although nowhere near the same caliber as Bava's supernatural shocker, Conde's creature feature is still a worthwhile low budget effort, thankfully saved from obscurity by Alpha Video.

the black cinema explosion. Granted, most of these films were ultimately produced by white producers who saw the opportunity to exploit a burgeoning market (which is where most of the 'exploitation' comes from in 'black exploitation,' regardless of the film's artistic intent or social relevance), but most of the revenue still came from an urban black audience who were desperate for films that starred people of color and—if they were lucky—actually spoke the language of their cultural esthetics, giving them a much deserved, long overdue sense of cultural pride.

Although seventies black cinema was by and large devoted to the immensely popular crime film (since this was a subject that, unfortunately, the inner city audiences dealt with on a daily basis), filmmakers toyed with other genres within the African American context as well. It was inevitable that producers and scriptwriters would attempt 'colorful' updatings of the horror film, trading in Dracula and Frankenstein's monster's pasty complexions for something a little more mocha. The works of Mary Shelley, Bram Stoker, and RL Stevenson were deconstructed to accommodate racial politics and monsters with a bit more 'soul'. Hollywood blockbusters like William Friedkin's *The Exorcist* (1974) were plagiarized, whereas others dealing with voodoo were blaxploitation efforts if only by default. By the time these Nubian creature features started picking up steam, black cinema (and independent drive-in cinema as a whole) was being edged out of the theatres by the Cineplex friendly multi million dollar extravaganzas being churned out of Hollywood which were also learning to diversify their casts.

Unfortunately, this subgenre never had much of an opportunity to evolve, although all black films have been making something of a comeback in recent years. With the close of the seventies, many of the barriers in cinema had been breached. Although blacks in mainstream films were still of-

Mamuwalde puts the bite on Dr. Welby, M.D. whilst Marvel puts the bite on black horror films. Cover art for *Spoof* V1#4 (March 1973)

ten employed in a token fashion, Hollywood was showing signs of progress when it came to diversifying their casts and to the roles being given to African Americans, even if it was a slow, uphill battle. Black cinema soon garnered a respect long since denied it by the mainstream with the likes of Spike Lee and John Singleton, but more exploitative efforts—horror films among them—would have little part in it. (There is a longstanding joke about token black characters in horror films, and how one can predict their chances of survival by the color of their skin. Having seen more than most, I can say that this bon mot is far from unfounded.)

During the eighties, most of the black creature features were re-released on video by companies like Xenon, who realized there was still a niche market for such films. (Xenon, though, had the

A very prophetic closure for "Blechhula!" from Spoof V1#4
March 1973) Marvel Comics Group

unpleasant habit of re-titling predominantly white films and masquerading them as black exploitation efforts. Al Adamson's *Nurse Sheri* [1977]—which had only two black actors in supporting roles—was re-released as *Black Voodoo*, and Paul Annett's *The Beast Must Die* [1974]—again, two actors shy of being colorless—bore the title *Black Werewolf*.) A few newer productions accompanied these re-releases, but these amateurish efforts were quickly lost amidst the glut of straight-to-video efforts cluttering the densely packed shelves of chain video stores. (There was even a hardcore sex effort, the 1987 quickie *Lust for Blackula*, which shows just how ingrained its inspiration was on the cinematic psyche.)

Not surprisingly, there was still a demand for cinema that featured strong black characters, and the occasional horror film would reflect this. *Def by Temptation* (1990), which featured a struggling

Samuel L Jackson, was a supernatural shocker featuring a predominantly African American cast. Bernard Rose's *Candyman* (1992)—as well as its two inferior sequels—succeeded if only because the sympathetic bogeyman was portrayed by Tony Todd (1954–), a versatile actor with a commanding presence who has almost made a career of supporting roles in horror and sci fi fare. Todd also stole the show in the Tom Savini remake of George A Romero's *Night of the Living Dead* (1990)—not an easy task, since he was filling the shoes of the late Duane Jones and vying for screen time with Tom Towles and Patricia Tallman.

The anthology *Tales from the Hood* (1995) placed the black horror film in a more modern urban environment, trading in psychedelic soul and platform shoes for hip hop and Converse high tops. Sadly, this film proved to be the final screen appearance of Rosalind Cash, who had already made her mark in the seventies with *The Omega Man* (1971) and *Dr Black, Mr Hyde* (1975).

The same year, black horror went mainstream with Wes Craven's *Vampire in Brooklyn* (1995), a vehicle for Eddie Murphy that rarely strayed from the comedian's established formula. The strongest black monster movie icon of the nineties, though, was Wesley Snipes' updating of Marvel Comics' *Blade* (1998), a half human vampire hunter whose antics would give Van Helsing a coronary. This melding of action and horror was popular enough to spawn two sequels before losing steam. Whether or not these primarily white, big budget shoot 'em ups with a twist truly qualify as black exploitation or even black cinema is up for debate.

There are some other examples of the subgenre's inability to fully give up the ghost, like Ernest R Dickerson's *Bones* (2001), a vengeance from beyond the grave flick starring rapper Snoop Dogg né Calvin Cordozar Broadus (1971–) as well as the undisputed queen of black exploitation films, Pam Grier.

The biggest push in the right direction was from Full Moon Video's 'new urban horrors' division, Alchemy Entertainment (which later became Big City Pictures). In the few years it was around, this label released a handful of horror films that featured predominantly black casts against inner city backdrops, including *Ragdoll* (1999), *Killjoy* (2000), *The Horrible Dr Bones* (2000) and *Cryptz* (2002). Alas, these films were in general poorly made outings that held little interest to discerning horror fans of any ethnicity, and thus were quickly relegated to the three for two bins at chain video stores. The trend continued, and although many of the films that followed were actually made by blacks, these productions were rarely any more competent or engaging.

We can only guess where the first wave of black horror films would have gone had they been given a fighting chance. Some of the films that followed would have fared just as poorly as their predecessors, transplanting black actors into already hackneyed scripts. As a whole, the subgenre would have likely evolved and explored the horror genre like any other culture, bringing to them very distinct idioms. We can see moments of that in some of these early black horror efforts, when the monster shucks off its shock for shock's sake rubber mask and reveals something deeper about its plight, but it is never sufficiently explored. (Except for *Ganja and Hess*, which—despite its cinematic shortcomings—transcends the conventions of the genre.) So, instead of crying over spilled milk, we will simply have to accept these films for what they are—admirable monster movies that did what they could with whatever means at their disposal—and groove on their low rent inner city charms.

Listen to the wisdom of a seven year old horror fan: if movie monsters can't have 'fros and be accompanied by funky theme music, then, really, what's the point?

ALTHOUGH I have made an exhaustive attempt to catalog and review all the productions that could be considered black exploitation horror films made during the seventies, I seriously doubt this list is complete. (The fact that it is classified as a subgenre—even though it is made up of a dozen films that spanned a five year stretch—is a subject worthy of discussion in and of itself.)

Two films often lumped in with the others, but which so far I have been unable to track down to confirm any associations, are Ray Marsh's *Lord Shango* (1975) and Barry Rosen's *Gang Wars* (1976) aka *The Devil's Express*. The former is supposedly a fairly serious and competent movie that deals with voodoo as a religion, but whether the proceedings are actually supernatural or not remains to be seen by yours truly. (It was released on videocassette under the misleading title of *The Color of Love* by Xenon Entertainment in 1991, but is now long out of print and nearly impossible to track down.) The latter is an exploitation film in every sense of the word—a low budget affair that thrusts a bloodthirsty Chinese demon into the middle of a war between rival street gangs in New York; it features a black lead, but its ties to the subgenre explored here may be tenuous.

Even more elusive is what *may* be a supernatural horror film from the seventies called *The Obsessed One*, but the poster is ambiguous. The first reference I found to it was in the wonderful book on the black film explosion, *What It Is...What It Was!* [Hyperion Books; 1998], and have since tracked down numerous copies of the one-sheet for sale online. Directed by Ramdjan Abdoelrahman—now a producer for Dutch television—and released by 21st Century Distribution, ads tout "The Bride Finally Died... Her Torture Ended. For Him, it was the Beginning of a Brutal, Savage Trail of Possessed Horror!"

Many other soul cinema historians would have undoubtedly included Cliff Roquemore's *Petey Wheatstraw* (1977) aka *The Devil's Son-in-Law*, but despite the supernatural lynchpins, this film is an *intentional* comedy. (Okay, so maybe it has more right being here than *The Thing with Two Heads*, but since the *only* moment of horror *Petey Wheatstraw* can lay claim to is Rudy Ray Moore accosting some poor kid on the street shouting "I'm gonna comb yo' nappy hair"—which he proceeds to do amidst cries of *real* pain—I had to make a judgment call.)

Some cineastes also include the Manuel Caño obscurity *Vudú Sangriento* [Bloody Voodoo] (1973) aka *Voodoo Black Exorcist*, but since this is a Spanish film that does not take place in urban America, I felt its exclusion self evident. Any other oversights are, well, just that.

Before commencing with the reviews, I need to address the inevitable concerns of some readers. Am I qualified to discuss horror and exploitation cinema? Sure. Am I qualified to discuss cinema created largely by and for African Americans? Of course not. I am no more qualified to discuss the black experience than a black person who grew up in urban America can adequately describe growing up white in white suburbia. I am ignorant by default, so all I can do is offer an outsider's perspective of the genre. (I'd like to think that the fact I regularly use no-lye relaxers like Ultra Sheen to straighten my own nappy hair gives me some insight into their plight, but that would just be wrong.)

ABBY (1974)

American International Pictures, Inc. [US] Mid America Pictures [US] DIR: William Brent Girdler PRO: William Brent Girdler, Mike Henry and Gordon Cornell Layne SCR: Gordon Cornell Layne DOP: William L Asman EXP: Samuel Z Arkoff MFX: Joe Kenney SFX: Samuel E Price MUS: Patti Henderson and Robert O Ragland STR: Brice Amos, William P Bradford (aka Bill Bradford), Chuck Broadus, Casey Brown, Terry Carter, Nathan Cook, Michael Coulden, Claude Fulkerson, Bobby Griffin, Don Henderson, Rhodi Hill, Joann Holcomb, Bob Holt, Robin James, Julia James, Felece Kinchelow, Charles Kissinger, Fletchen Kwanstic, William Marshall, John Miller, Mary Minor, Elliott Moffitt, Joanna Moore, Nancy Lee Owens, Joan Ray, George Robinson, Carolyn Stewart (aka Carol Speed), Austin Stoker and Bill Wilson
AKA: *Possess My Soul*
    Seduccion Diabolica [Diabolic Seduction]
Approximately 89m; Color; Rated R
ADL: "Abby Doesn't Need a Man Anymore... The Devil is Her Lover Now!"

DR GARNET WILLIAMS (William Marshall), a professor of theology and archeology, decides to do a little excavating in the mother country, and accidentally unleashes the spirit of the African devil god Eshu (Gesundheit). Meanwhile, his daughter in law Abby (Carol Speed née Stewart) and her family move into a new home which, they find out on the night of their housewarming, harbors an unseen force that has it in for their furniture.

Things start getting *really* weird when Abby gets all hot and bothered preparing some poultry for dinner, but—publicly—starts turning heads with her newfound social awkwardness towards her friends and fellow churchgoers. (She throws up all over one parishioner, and another she promises to "take upstairs and fuck the shit out of" in front of the man's fiancée.) When she isn't acting like a monkey in heat (that's not a racial slur, I assure you) or playing merry-go-round with an old cracker with a bad ticker, she's sleazing her way from one nightclub to the next, her concerned husband, the esteemed Reverend Williams (Terry Carter), always one step behind.

As either horror or exploitation, *Abby* is not a noteworthy effort. The film is, however, notorious for the fact that Warner Brothers sued American International Pictures and director Girdler for copyright infringement. Although not quite the note-for-note remake that many sources claim, *Abby* does bear a marked resemblance to William Friedkin's *The Exorcist*, enough so that the folks at Warner took them to court and forced a cease and desist on any future release of the film. According to the posthumously official William Girdler website www.williamgirdler.com:

> *Warner Brothers and Sam Arkoff of AIP struck a bargain in which Warner Brothers would release the frozen revenue generated by the film to Girdler and company. In return, Arkoff and Mid America agreed never to air or distribute the film without Warner Brothers' permission. Girdler saw no profits from the film. The case was settled a few weeks before he died.*

Abby—made on $100,000—raked in somewhere between $4-9m during its abbreviated theatrical release in the States, outgrossing *Blac-*

US advertisement herald for
Abby (1974) American International Pictures, Inc.

ula. (The total box office receipts differ between sources, and it wasn't unheard of for both AIP and Girdler to exaggerate the profits in order to impress theatres as well as potential investors.)

Having never been legitimately available on home video, it is no surprise that the lucky few who have actually seen it either caught it during its original theatrical run, or plunked down twenty bucks (or much, *much* more, in some cases) for a washed out, grainy bootleg. (Curiously enough, when MGM Home Entertainment bought the rights to AIP's back catalog for its Midnite Movies line of DVD releases, *Abby* wasn't included in the package.) Unfortunately, this is one of those efforts that is more impressive as a lost film than, well, a found one.

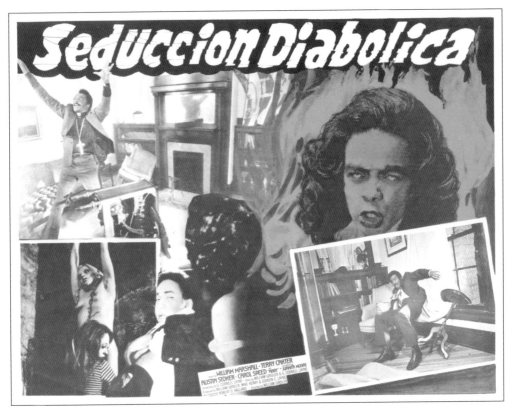

Mexican lobby card for Abby (1974) American International Pictures, Inc./Mid-America Pictures

At the risk of losing my esteemed position as trash film connoisseur (he said, with tongue firmly in cheek), it appears that I may be the only person of this camp who felt cheated by the experience of actually having seen it. Although a reviewer for the *New York Times* called it "an effective and chilling film," I found it laughable. Although *Abby* holds a place in the top twenty list of many trash horror enthusiasts, I wasn't laughing when I should have been.

More to the point, *Abby* makes Italian imports like Alberto de Martino's *L'Antichristo* (1974) and Ovidio Assoniti's *Chi Sei?* (1974) seem palatable. The drama prior to the initial shocks comes across as a string of television commercials stripped of any product references (although one would swear that a sequence used later on in the film was pilfered from a Jesus Christ of Latter Day Saints ad spot). Scenes of horror are offered without any build up, and the events seem to leave little if any lasting impression on the players whatsoever. Although *Abby* even goes so far as to copy *The Exorcist*'s Captain Howdy subliminals (here, the demon is portrayed by Speed sporting a bald cap, ugly teeth and *really* big eyebrows), the screenwriters do take the final confrontation between good and evil out of the bedroom and put it where it rightly belongs: in a nightclub.

Speed's performance is embarrassing (methinks she may have had a bigger hand in suppressing this film than Warner Brothers, but don't quote me on that), but then again, she had the material and its handling working against her. Marshall (1924–2003) goes through the motions, but then again, who could blame him. (Granted, horror fans will be hard pressed to see him as anything besides Blacula, and since this film is an obvious drop from both that film and its sequel, why make the effort?) Marshall never had a good word to say about this film; although he felt that it didn't delve far enough into African culture (among other legitimate gripes), Speed claims he hated *Abby* "because [her] photo was the one associated with the success of *Abby*" and not his. Stoker (1943–) seems to come out better than the other performers, but then he's sadly underused, so doesn't suffer nearly as many indignations as everyone else involved. Considering the talented cast at the filmmaker's disposal—all of whom deserved far, far better—I just couldn't bring myself to laugh.

When he died in a helicopter crash in the Philippines at the premature age of thirty, director Girdler (1947–78) had nine films to his credit, six of which were horror—the underrated Ed Gein inspired shocker *Three on a Meathook* among them—and three of which were black exploitation efforts, including the fun Pam Grier vehicle *Sheba, Baby* (1975). (He was also responsible for scoring the JG Patterson Jr 1974 Z-grade gore effort, *The Body Shop*. No one who has seen the film, though, will consider it a feather in the cap.)

Composer Ragland (1931–) made a career out of scoring B-grade horror fare during the seventies—*The Touch of Satan* (1970), *The Thing with Two Heads* (1973) and *Mansion of the Doomed* (1977) topping the list—but eventually worked his way 'up' to B-grade action films in the decades that followed.

As The Fearmonger, actor Charles Kissinger (1925–91)—who appeared in all but two of Girdler's films—hosted the prime time horror program *Fright Night* (1971–75), which aired Saturday evenings on WDRB TV-41 in Louisville, Kentucky. In addition to playing the resident can-

nibal in *Three on a Meathook* (1972), he also did the voiceover on several ad spots for the film.

Sadly, the cinematic career of Speed (1945–) barely lasted nine years, which included a supporting role in Jack Hill's women in prison classic *The Big Bird Cage* (1972) and came to a screeching halt when she played opposite Rudy Ray Moore in blaxploitation's last gasp, *The Disco Godfather* (1979). (This film also marked the end of Moore's acting career.) The versatile actress had some success on syndicated television, and even performed one of her own musical compositions for the soundtrack of *Abby*. Not to be usurped by the cast and crew of Friedkin's *The Exorcist*, Speed has claimed that the set of *Abby* was also plagued by inexplicable, thus supernatural, goings on. If only the filmmakers had captured some of this 'bona fide' poltergeist activity on film, *Abby* may have created the ripples it intended.

BLACK THE RIPPER (1974)

FRSCO/Frisco Productions Ltd [US] DIR: Frank R Saletri PRO: Frank R Saletri SCR: Frank R Saletri STR: Dale E Bach, Pearl Elizabeth Dobbins (aka Liz Renay), Marva Farmer, Renata Harmon, Joe Marsh, Bole Nikoli and Hugh van Patten
Running time unknown; Color; Unrated

IT IS STILL unknown whether this film is lost, or if it actually ever reached post production; aside from some rumors of sightings, the only evidence of its existence is from an advertisement that ran in *Variety* magazine in 1974. (Most online sources list the film as 1975, but neither date has been verified to my satisfaction.) Since there is no print available for review purposes, this inclusion will be predictably brief.

I think it is safe for us to assume that the clever title speaks for itself. Three of the actors— Dale E Bach, Pearl Dobbins (née Renay) and

Marva Farmer—appeared the previous year in *Blackenstein*. (Although Renay is listed in most credits, when asked about *Black the Ripper* in a recent interview, she insists she was never asked to participate in the project, much less heard of it.) What few credits are available were obtained from online sources (the most complete being from *The Encyclopedia of Fantastic Film & Television*), and from these few credits we know it *must* be a masterpiece of the genre. Why? Because the man singlehandedly responsible for it is none other than Frank R Saletri, the producer-cum-scriptwriter of *Blackenstein*.

So, all of you cinephiles out there reading this, listen up: quit wasting your time trying to unearth a copy of the elusive Lon Chaney vehicle *London After Midnight* (1927) and get cracking on *this* number. If this film does indeed exist, it must be found. Not only will this forgotten treasure change the way we look at black horror fare, it will ensure you a footnote in the annals of film history. C'mon, who remembers Chaney anyway; this is *Black the Ripper* we're talking about here!

Me? I'll be pawing through the basements of forgotten movie houses looking for the Tod Browning film, while you simpletons are looking for a wretched slasher flick that probably doesn't even exist. Hey, I'm the one who has to review the films, after all, so call it an act of self preservation.

How can I make such assumptions about the alleged film's worth, having never even seen Saletri's script? Read ahead…

BLACKENSTEIN (1973)

FRSCO/Frisco Productions Ltd [US] DIR: William A Levey PRO: Frank R Saletri SCR: Frank R Saletri DOP: Robert Caramico EXP: Ted Tetrick MFX: Gordon Freed and William Munns SFX: Kenneth Strickfaden MUS: Cardella de Milo and Lou Frohman STR: Dale E Bach, Nick Bolin, Don Brodie, Bob Brophy, Andy C, James Cousar, Cardella de Milo, Joe de Sue, Pearl Elizabeth Dobbins (aka Liz Renay), Marva Farmer, Daniel Fauré, Beverly Haggerty (aka Beverly Hagerty), John Hart, Robert L Hurd, Roosevelt Jackson, Andrea King, Karin Lind, Yvonne Robinson, Gerald Soucie (aka Jerry Soucie) and Ivory Stone
AKA: *(The) Black Frankenstein*
      Blackstein
      Frankenstein Negro [Black Frankenstein]
      Return of Blackenstein
Approximately 87m; Color; Rated R
DVD: *Blackenstein* [Xenon Video; 87m; FS; NTSC R1]
VHS: *Blackenstein* [Media Entertainment; 87m; FS; NTSC] [Xenon Video; 87m; FS; NTSC]
ADL: "Not Since Frankenstein Stalked the Earth has the World Known so Terrifying a Day… or Night"

DR WINIFRED WALKER (Ivory Stone) shows up on the doorstep of her former teacher Dr Stein (who, we are told, won the Nobel Peace Prize for cracking the DNA code), hoping he can help her fiancé, Eddie (Joe de Sue), who lost both of his arms and legs to a landmine in Vietnam. The renowned scientist (John Hart) performs a quick limb transplant then injects the sullen Purple Heart with a heavy dose of DNA (I guess he didn't have enough of his own); luckily, Eddie doesn't grow a zebra leg like one of the mad doctor's other, less fortunate, human guinea pigs. Things are looking up until Winifred rejects the advances of the doctor's Nubian assistant Malcolm (Roosevelt Jackson), who extols revenge by sabotaging the procedure. Eddie promptly regresses into a throwback with a prominent brow and flattop afro, and goes on the expected killing spree, first going after an abusive male nurse, then any helpless woman who stumbles into his path.

Although a little too slow to make the ranks of the So Bad It's Great Hall Of Shame, *Blackenstein* is still one doozey of a rotten film that will appeal only to the prurient interests of hardcore trashfiends with whom patience is not an issue. Fettered by bad acting, a lousy script and dime store set pieces (note the hydrogen peroxide bottle with 'DNA' scrawled in felt marker on its face), this ranks as one of the most inept entries in soul cinema's horror cycle, vying with Girdler's *Abby* for the lowest rung. Whereas *Abby* is a tad more competent—especially in respect to the performances—*Blackenstein* proves to be the funnier of the two films if only because one goes in with only the lowest of expectations.

Unable to deliver simple lines—let alone emote—the actors sleepwalk from one scene to the next, and it isn't hard to imagine them napping on the sidelines when a camera isn't trained on them. (Eddie and his one-expression-fits-every-occasion delivery implore the viewer to wonder if the poor vet wouldn't be better off employed as a doorstop, since the landmine apparently did a number on his personality as well.) The script, besides being hack reiteration, is festooned with meaningless, migraine inducing scientific gibberish. Dr Stein's laboratory looks like something from an Al Adamson flick, for good reason: what wasn't salvaged from forty year old Universal monster movies was probably purchased from a local novelty shop on clearance. (Strickfadden was responsible for the gadgetry used in the original 1931 version of *Frankenstein* and its sequels, and much of his 'electrifying' props were recycled by such low rent exercises as this and *Dracula vs Frankenstein* [1971] during the early seventies.) Whenever showing the supposedly limbless vet, the effects department thought it unnecessary to conceal the fact that the statuesque actor did indeed have arms and legs, and simply threw a sheet over him. (Really, how hard would it have been to cut holes in the bed or gurney before filming these scenes? As if someone wouldn't *notice* the size fourteen wide tents made by his feet.) The day for night sequences could never be

White or black, you'll scream, too, when you first catch sight of the monster's tragic hair-don't. US pressbook advertisement for Blackenstein (1973) FRSCO/Frisco Productions Ltd.

mistaken for anything but that, and the sound engineer apparently pilfered everything he could from the original *Star Trek* sound effects library. Worst of all, the theme song displays not one lick of a wah-wah pedal; no self respecting black exploitation film would be caught dead without a wakka-wakka drenched credits sequence, thus forcing one to question *Blackenstein's* soul cinema appellation.

The movie has a higher sleaze quotient than its peers, at least during the last few reels, with some gratuitous nudity and primitive gore that is just shy of HG Lewis' patented carnage. (Most of the creature's scantily clad victims are eviscerated, and

FRANKENSTEIN NEGRO
UNA TERRIBLE PESADILLA QUE SE CONVIERTE
EN UNA PAVOROSA REALIDAD!!...

LO ESTREMECERA DE TERROR!

Mexican lobby card for Blackenstein (1973) FRSCO/Frisco Productions Ltd.

he himself is torn apart by a pack of police dogs, although the aftermath proves to be little more than shots of trained Dobermans picking pieces of liver off the fallen monster's jacket.) Had the laughable excesses been introduced earlier on, *Blackenstein* would have proven more cult worthy. But as it stands, every scene is dragged out twice as long as necessary, and the stretches without dialogue are almost as mind numbing as the droning exchanges one waits anxiously for throughout.

Of course, any one of the titles applied to this flick is a misnomer because our resident mad scientist is *not* black. The monster is, but any self respecting horror fan knows the monster was *never* named Frankenstein. So, a better title would have been "Dr Frankenstein's Black Monster". But

then, this film's doctor is actually named Stein, and his patchwork creature is not so much black as sepia, but using a color coded system to determine ethnicity may be considered racist, so "Dr Stein's African American Monster" would be not only be more apropos but also politically correct, methinks. So... screw it. It's a man made monster with a flattop afro named Blackenstein, so take it or leave it.

Director Levey has to his credit a number of low budget genre efforts, all bad. The lesser of the evils—this, sadly, and the nudie cutie *Wham, Bam, Thank You Spaceman* (1975)—are overshadowed by the likes of *The Happy Hooker goes to Washington* (1977) and his cinematic last gasp *Hellgate* (1989), a production that can only justify its existence by being the one film with enough guts to cast an underappreciated Ron Palillo in the lead. (Being typecast as Horshack in *Welcome Back, Kotter* is enough to disable anyone's career. But I digress…)

Saletri (1928–82) was a criminal lawyer who was murdered gangland style in a mansion he owned that had once belonged to Bela Lugosi. Two of his projects that never got off the ground were screenplays he had written: *Sherlock Holmes in the Adventure of the Golden Vampire*—which was to have starred shock rocker Alice Cooper as Dracula—and *Sherlock Holmes in the Adventures of the Werewolf of the Baskervilles.*

After getting his start on the Ed Wood scripted horror nudie *Orgy of the Dead* (1965), cinematographer Caramico went on to an illustrious career lensing such Oscar nominees as *Octaman* (1971), *Lemora: A Child's Tale of the Supernatural* (1973), *Eaten Alive* (1977) and *Spawn of the Slithis* (1978). Hey, he's an artist in *my* book.

Co-star Liz Renay née Dobbins (1926–)—ex-gangster moll and award winning Marilyn Monroe lookalike—has a couple dozen exploitation films to her credit, not the least of which are Ray Dennis Steckler's *The Thrill Killers* (1964) and John Waters' *Desperate Living* (1977). In recent years, she appeared in the two latest Steckler abominations, namely *The Corpse Grinders 2* and *Mark of the Astro-Zombies* (both 2000). More than likely, the people behind *Blackenstein* sought only to capitalize on her name, as she is given only a few minutes of screen time, and then just long enough to fill out a flimsy negligee with her D cups and get eviscerated by our sexually confused monster. Still, she gave it her all… and more. As a publicity stunt, the well endowed actress streaked down Hollywood Boulevard during the opening night of Levey's film. Now *that's* what I call dedication to one's art.

Okay, folks, it's all uphill from here. I promise.

BLACULA (1972)

American International Pictures, Inc. [US] DIR: William Crain PRO: Joseph T Naar SCR: Raymond Koenig and Joan Torres DOP: John M Stevens EXP: Samuel Z Arkoff SFX: Roger George MUS: Gene Page and Various Artists SND: Blacula [RCA/Victor; 33m; LP] [Razor & Tie Records; 33m; CD] STR: Eric Brotherson, Elisha Cook Jr, Ji-Tu Cumbuka, Logan Field, Ted Harris, Ketty Lester, Charles Macaulay, William Marshall, Vonetta McGee, Rick Metzler, Denise Nicholas, Gordon Pinsent, Thalmus Rasulala, Lance Taylor Sr. and Emily Yancy

AKA: *Blacula, Le Vampire Noir* [Blacula, The Black Vampire]
Dracula Negro [Black Dracula]
El Vampiro Negro [The Black Vampire]
De Zwarte Vampier [The Black Vampire]
Approximately 92m; Color; Rated PG

DVD: *Blacula* [MGM Home Entertainment; 93(92)m; WS; NTSC R1]

VHS: *Blacula* [MGM Home Entertainment; 93(92)m; FS; NTSC][Thorn EMI/HBO Video; 92m; FS; NTSC]

ADL: "He's Black! He's Beautiful! He's Blacula!"

IN 1780, African prince Mamuwalde (William Marshall) makes a social visit to Castle Dracula to implore the Transylvanian Count to put an end to the slave trade. Unfortunately for him, his wife, and subjugated brothers and sisters, Dracula (Charles Macaulay) not only has no desire to free his people ("Slavery has merit, I believe," he says pointedly), he also decides to initiate Mamuwalde into the ranks of the undead. Mockingly dubbing the prince 'Blacula,' he then seals him up in a coffin where he languishes in a secret chamber for over 200 years.

Jump cut to 1972. A couple of opportunistic antique dealers lay their limp wrists on Dracula's estate and unknowingly ship the imprisoned prince to the United States. Freed of his chains (subtle, that), the undead Mamuwalde employs a

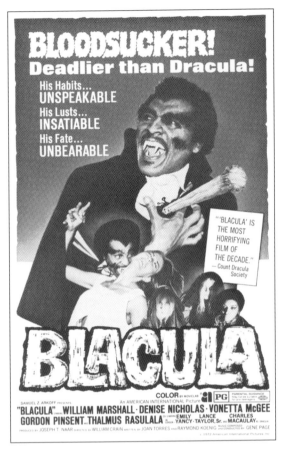

US pressbook cover art for Blacula (1972)
American International Pictures, Inc.

this very seriously, and that the rest of the crew adapted the self same attitude before all was said and done. Opening with a tacky animated credits sequence that borders on the surreal, we are also treated to some long in-the-tooth vampires that would give their Filipino counterparts a run for their money (good thing the actors weren't required to speak), exploding oil lamps (who the heck needs hand grenades when there's some kerosene handy), and some of the worst dancers this side of American Bandstand (the casting department must have searched far and wide to find the only black people in Hollywood without a lick of soul).

And the dialogue is priceless. When the body of one of Blacula's flamboyant victims disappears from the morgue, a lieutenant detective asks, "Who the hell would want a dead faggot?" (Good thing they only hire the sensitive ones to fill these positions of power.) When the film's hero goes to examine the body of another victim and discovers what appear to be two tiny pinpricks on the neck, the mortician comments on how the "flesh was torn right out in a big chunk."

Undeniably, Blacula's one truly saving grace is the presence of William Marshall as the titular bloodsucker, who was a spry fifty years of age when this film was made. Boasting a commanding stage presence not unlike that of James Earl Jones (his imposing 6'5" stature and deep voice only further the comparison), Marshall gives the film a credibility it would otherwise lack. The fact that his portrayal of the sympathetic antihero is in the same vein as Dark Shadows' Barnabas Collins only goes to make him more sympathetic in his plight. (It comes as little surprise that Marshall had a hand in developing the background of the character for the film, even though he's not given any credit for changing Blacula from a stereotypical jive talking brother to an African aristocrat.)

couple of henchmen and sets up house in Los Angeles. He becomes obsessed with a young woman who is the spitting image of his long dead princess, Luva (Vonetta McGee). And of course, in true lovelorn vampire fashion, nothing will stand in the way of him reclaiming his reincarnated bride, even a savvy doctor (Thalmus Rasulala) who has seen Mamuwalde's, uhm, *dark* side.

I absolutely adored this film when I was, oh, about seven, and thirty years later I still find it appealing, although not as I did when I was of a more easily impressionable age. Production values are overall passable, but one gets the impression that the scriptwriters weren't taking any of

US pre-release advertisement for Blacula (1972) American International Pictures, Inc.

Unfortunately (or fortunately, if you can see the humor in it), Marshall is difficult to take seriously when he is overcome with bloodlust; the term 'ugly on a stick' just doesn't do justice to the bushy eyebrows and even funkier sideburns that complete his vampiric alter ego.

Co-star Rasulala also does an admirable job playing it straight, and keeps Marshall from completely stealing the show.

Although the film never reaches its potential as exceptional horror fare or social commentary, it stands alone. *Blacula* is recognized as the first truly black monster movie, and since no other has given us an icon as powerful as Prince Mamuwalde, the film has become the poster child for the very trend it started. But because no one else could replicate its strengths or repeat its longstanding success in the dog eat dog world of drive-in cinema, this trend soon died.

This film was proclaimed Best Horror Film of 1972 by the Academy of Horror & Sci Fi Films. Despite this honorable achievement, *Blacula* will forever hold its head in shame for immortalizing—to the horror of future generations unfamiliar with seventies pop culture—the largest collar ever to grace a pink polyester shirt.

Crain spent much of his time helming episodes of such televised crime dramas as *The Mod Squad* (1968–73), *S.W.A.T.* (1975–76) and *Starsky and Hutch* (1975–79). Star Marshall (1924–2003), who was trained as a Shakespearean stage actor, had a sporadic film career from 1952 to 1996. His longest stint was playing the King of Cartoons on *Pee-Wee's Playhouse* (1986–90). The *Sunday Times* once hailed Marshall as "the best Othello of our time," which shouldn't surprise anyone in the least. Co-star Rasulala had a few other notable black exploitation films

Mexican lobby card for Blacula (1972) Warner Brothers

to his credit, including the Pam Grier offerings *Bucktown* and *Friday Foster* (both 1975). (In the former, he played a heavy opposite Fred Williamson, and the two of them got to duke it out in one of the best, most realistically choreographed fight scenes to be found in a low budget crime flick.) Prior to her regular appearances in *Cagney & Lacey* (1982–88) and *L.A. Law* (1986–94), McGee (1940–) also appeared in *Shaft in Africa* and *Detroit 9000* (both 1973). Having appeared in such classic film noir efforts as *The Maltese Falcon* (1941), lovable character actor Cook (1903–95) graced with his twitchy presence such shockers as *Voodoo Island* (1957) and *House on Haunted Hill* (1959).

And let's not forget the groovy soundtrack by Page (1939–98), which was thankfully saved

from obscurity when it was re-issued on CD in 1998. (Also included in the mix are three numbers written and produced by The Hues Corporation.) If early seventies action movie style funk is your bag, this score comes highly recommended by yours truly.

Some lucky theatregoers were given a Vampire Protection Kit: a printed envelope containing an informative insert and a baggie of dried leaves from the "Transylvanian Bat-Laurel tree", which one is instructed to "thumbtack over your door or window" or "wear it on your breast pocket" so that "no one but you and Blacula will know that you are being protected". No, Virginia, there is no Transylvanian Bat-Laurel tree, so I guess patrons were just shit out of luck.

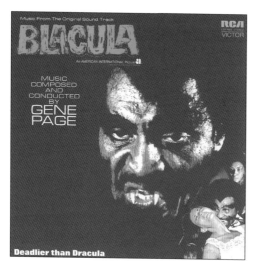

US soundtrack LP for Blacula (1972)
RCA/Victor Records #LSP-4806

Dr Black, Mr Hyde (1975)

Dimension Pictures [US] Hyde Productions
[US] DIR: William Crain PRO: Charles Walker
SCR: Larry le Bron DOP: Tak Fujimoto EXP:
Manfred Bernhard MFX: Stan Winston SFX:
Harry Wollman MUS: Johnny Pate STR: Marc
Alaimo, Roma Alvarez, Judith Angeline, Bobby
Angelle, Gregory Awoskia, Manfred Bernhard, Buff
Brady, Wilson Bryant III, Bernard Terry Casey (aka
Bernie Casey), Rosalind Cash, Angel Colbert, Ji-Tu
Cumbuka, Cora Lee Day, Janet Dey, Stu Gilliam,
Shirley Harding, LaVerne Jackson, Gwyn Karon,
Milt Kogan, Sam Laws, Joy Lee, Val Loring, Virginia
Lynne, Gene Massey, Nancy Middleton, Bob Minor,
Sam Nudell, Marie O'Henry, Joseph W Reynolds,
Adrian Ricard, Elizabeth Robinson, Phillip Roye,
Pamela Serpe, Daniel Spelling, Rai Tasco, Della
Thomas, Kejo Thomas and Erik Washington
AKA: *Decision for Doom*
  Dr Black and Mr Hyde
  Dr Black and Mr White
  El Demonio Negro [The Black Demon]
  Das Monster von London [The Monster of
  London]
  The Watts Monster
Approximately 87m; Color; Rated R

VHS: *Dr Black, Mr Hyde* [United Home Video;
88(87)m; FS; NTSC] [VCI Home Video; 88(87)m;
FS; NTSC]
ADL: "A Monster He Can't Control… Has Taken
Over His Very Soul!"

DRIVEN BY the death of his mother, a maid at
a brothel who succumbed to liver damage, award
winning scientist Dr Henry Pride (Bernie Casey)
has developed a serum with remarkable regen-
erative qualities. Still in the experimental stages,
Pride tries out his elixir on a black mouse, which
immediately sheds its pigmentation and takes
out its frustration on its fellow lab rats. A patient
on the critical list becomes the next guinea pig—
much to the chagrin of the doctor's main squeeze
Dr Worth (Rosalind Cash)—and gives new
meaning to the word 'spook' before cashing in her
chips. Not wanting to risk any more lives, Pride
takes a whack at his new wonder drug, living up
to the endearingly contrived title and taking out
his repressed anger on the prostitutes whom he
blames for the death of his alcoholic mother.

Dr Black, Mr Hyde is one of the slicker black
exploitation horror efforts, and boasts some exceptional performances. As William Marshall
did for *Blacula*, Bernie Casey does for *Dr Black,
Mr Hyde*: the lead actor brings a level of respect-
ability to the material that might otherwise be
absent, and instills in the character much needed
pathos. But not unlike *Blacula*, the viewer can't
help but feel that these performers are being re-
duced in some way by their participation. (Mr
Hyde's makeup isn't nearly as silly looking as
Dracula's Nubian peer, but he also isn't nearly as
intimidating. Maybe it's the partially frosted afro,
I don't know.) Interestingly, the combination of
prosthetics coupled with Casey's performance as
Hyde reminds one of Howard Sherman's portrayal of zombie mascot Bub in George Romero's
Day of the Dead (1985). His cries of rage and
confusion are those of a problematic child, and

VHS box art for Dr. Black, Mr. Hyde (Circa 1985)
United Home Video #6201

one expects him to start drooling profusely during his tantrums.

Since *Blacula* fell somewhat short as social commentary, director Crain does his best to make up for his previous oversight. Unfortunately, he and his cohorts overcompensate in their efforts. The racial issues prove to be far too heavy handed at times, as the very crux of the film will attest. Furthermore, their depictions of 'model' African Americans are often just as two dimensional as the stereotypical pitfalls they strive to avoid. (Naming the doctors Pride and Worth are only two of the not very subtle touches used to elevate the characters.) Had they chosen a more humanistic approach—as was applied in Crain's previous film—the messages in *Dr Black, Mr Hyde*

wouldn't be so easy to write off at times. Unfortunately, such balances are difficult to achieve, especially within the context of an exploitation film.

Handling of politics aside, this flick is not without its grievances. Sure, science is rarely an issue in such creature features, but no one makes any attempt to explain why the Hyde-juice turns people white as a sheet and gives them a Neanderthalian brow. But that's okay, because we—the viewers—can accept this as yet another of life's mysteries; it's better they leave it vague than bog down the script with even *more* bad science. What we *cannot* accept is that everyone—black or white—who gets up close and personal with Dr Pride's pissy alter ego mistakes him for Caucasian. I'm sorry, but white greasepaint and bleached contact lenses make him look no more like a honky than shoe polish would make yours truly look like a brother.

Dr Black, Mr Hyde has a low sleaze quotient considering the R rating. There is some nudity, but it is hardly gratuitous, and there is no gore to speak of. Shocks are few, but a scene involving an old woman who is subjected to the doctor's experiments is somewhat unnerving. (If only they had gotten *her* to run around in makeup, attacking the populace, the film may have been able to dish up some real scares.) And in a scene that almost seems to be a nod to *Blackenstein*, authorities once again try to take down the monster with police dogs; whereas Stein's patchwork creation was conveniently disassembled by the Dobermans, Mr Hyde makes short work of the German Shepherd sent after him. (The film follows this up with an almost surreal pastiche of *King Kong*'s tragic finale, and has Hyde face off a slew of officers from the top of a Gaudí-esque interpretation of the Empire State Building.)

Star Bernie Casey (1939–) was a former pro football player (1961–68) whose screen debut was *Guns of the Magnificent Seven* in 1969. Aside from *Dr Black, Mr Hyde*, his only real genre credits are two made for television horror flicks, *Gargoyles* (1972) (in which he also spent considerable time in Stan Winston's makeup chair) and *It Happened at Lakewood Manor* (1977) aka *Ants!* He is currently the Chairman of the Board of Trustees at the Savannah College of Art and Design. Co-star Cash (1938–95) probably had a feeling of déjà vu whilst on the set of *Dr Black, Mr Hyde* as she fought a whole cadre of melanin deficient African Americans in the big budget exploitation film *The Omega Man* (1971), which put something of a racial spin on Richard Matheson's *I Am Legend*. Fujimoto, now a highly respected cinematographer in Hollywood, got his start in exploitation flicks during the mid seventies, most notably with such Corman produced cult flicks as *Caged Heat* (1974) and *Death Race 2000* (1975).

I don't think this is quite what Robert Louis Stevenson had in mind, but who are we to judge?

Ganja and Hess (1972)

Kelly Jordan Enterprises, Inc. [US] DIR: William Gunn Jr (aka Bill Gunn) DIR: Efim Novikov (aka Fima Noveck, aka FH Noveck) PRO: Chiz Schultz SCR: William Gunn Jr (aka Bill Gunn) DOP: James E Hinton EXP: Jack Jordan and Quentin Kelly MUS: Sam Waymon STR: Betty Barney, Marlene Clark, Enrico Fales, Tara Fields, William Gunn Jr (aka Bill Gunn), Richard Harrow, John Hoffmeister, Leonard Jackson, Duane L Jones, Mabel King, Tommy Lane, Candece Tarpley, Betsy Thurman, Sam Waymon and the congregation of the Evangel Revivaltime Church
AKA: *Black Evil*
    Black Vampire
    Blackout: The Moment of Terror
    Blood Couple
    Double Possession
    Vampires of Harlem

Approximately 110m; Color; R
DVD: *Ganja & Hess* [All Day Entertainment; 110m; WS; NTSC R1]
VHS: *Black Evil* [Lettuce Entertainment; 78m; NTSC] *Black Vampire* [Impulse Productions; 78m; NTSC] *Blackout: The Moment of Terror* [Fantasy Video; 92(78)m; NTSC] *Blood Couple* [United American Video; 78m; NTSC] [Video Gems; 78m; NTSC]
ADL: "Some Marriages are made in Heaven. Others are made in Hell."

DR HESS GREEN (Duane Jones), a wealthy and highly respected anthropologist, comes to be in possession of an ancient dagger while studying the ancient civilization of Myrthia in Africa. His new research assistant, George 'I'm neurotic, okay?' Meda (Bill Gunn), goes ape shit one evening while staying over and tries to axe his boss in his sleep. During the scuffle, Meda stabs his host—presumably to death—with the 'diseased' pigsticker before taking his own life with a gun. Dr Green curiously survives the attack, but finds himself stricken with an unexpected thirst and wastes little time in lapping his guest's blood off the bathroom floor. Unfulfilled by the handy packets of red stuff he is later forced to pilfer from low income clinics, he soon acquires a taste for something a little fresher, conveniently supplied by unwary prostitutes.

In the midst of his newfound bloodlust, Meda's widow arrives from Amsterdam, having tracked her apparently AWOL hubby to Hess' doorstep. Unaware of George's fate, she wastes no time in committing some extracurricular infidelity with the brooding Hess, who has decided he no longer wants to be alone in his affliction. Inevitably, Ganja soon discovers her hubby's freezer burnt corpse, which Hess has stashed in the basement. After throwing a tantrum, she quickly accepts the loss and decides to marry her presumably psychotic host, unaware that he has plans to initiate her into his world of dependency.

US one-sheet poster art for Ganja and Hess (1973)
Kelly-Jordan Enterprises, Inc.

In 1972, Gunn was hired by executive producers Kelly and Jordan to film a black vampire film, hoping to cash in on *Blacula*'s success. (Prior to this, Jordan had produced a Swedish film for black audiences called *Georgia, Georgia*, scripted by Maya Angelou. Following *Ganja and Hess*, the only other film they managed to get released was Michael Schultz's hastily made action film *Honeybaby, Honeybaby*, released two years later.)

Gunn fulfilled his part of the bargain, and the producers premiered it in New York with much reluctance. In light of its poor reception—due in part to a lack of promotion—Kelly and Jordan pulled the film from theatres after only a week, and hired Novikov (1917–2004) to rework *Ganja and Hess* into something more market-able. Not only does his version run twenty two minutes shorter, it also includes some footage not found in Gunn's cut, all outtakes. Reportedly, the director was so incensed that, during a business meeting that followed the 're-envisioning' of his work, the enraged filmmaker threw a chair out of the producer's window.

This affront was released first as *Blood Couple*—to very little applause—and then again a year later as *Double Possession*, hoping to take advantage of *The Exorcist*'s success. It failed to garner an audience its second time out as well. Gunn took his cut of the film to the 1973 Cannes Film Festival, where it received a standing ovation from the audience. Despite the reception, *Ganja and Hess* would soon be pulled from circulation and become the stuff of cinematic legend. Novikov's edit, on the other hand, has remained in the public's discerning eye ever since, thanks to a number of low rent video companies who specialized in the public domain and took advantage of disputes over the film's ownership.

Ganja and Hess is a cult film and hailed as an underground classic by critics usually unreceptive to horror fare. It is without doubt the only black horror film to transcend the subgenre and avoid the conventions inherent in it. Unfortunately, in the eyes of this humble reviewer, *Ganja and Hess* has too many failings to qualify as a masterpiece. A gem in the rough, yes, but not a masterpiece.

Although he made a name for himself as a writer and actor, Gunn was first and foremost an artist, one of tremendous vision and talent. To deny this would be a fool's errand. But herein lies the problem: having a strong vision does not necessarily make one a good filmmaker. His eye for the visual was painterly, and his skills as a writer were unquestionable; his ability to mold them into a cohesive whole, however, was flawed. Like many 'art' films, attempts to reconcile two very different mediums often fail, the end result being

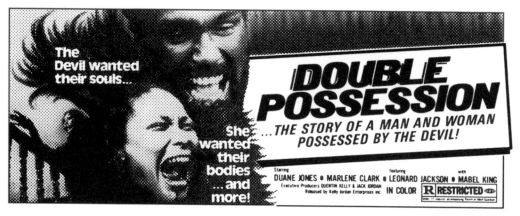

US pressbook advertisement for the re-release of Ganja and Hess (1974) Kelly-Jordan Enterprises, Inc.

ating something exciting by defying conventional cinema, or by making an accessible product that rebukes trends and offers something of lasting importance—are few and far between, as many, like Gunn, are crushed beneath the wheels of the Hollywood machine before they can reach this balance, precarious as it may be.

As a triumph of vision, *Ganja and Hess* succeeds. As a film, it displays flashes of brilliance but is often crushed by the weight of its own aspirations and Gunn's limitations to adapt to this new medium. The filmmakers cause unnecessary confusion from frame one, when we are told—vaguely—of the plight of our main character, presented as if this has already happened and what follows picks up from the already established storyline. Thirty minutes in, we realize that we may now be seeing those events unfold, but there is uncertainty. Discombobulated by the frustrating ambiguities, the viewer is distracted from the meat of the movie—Gunn's innovative take on vampirism and his commentaries on African American culture—and may be too quick to write it off as amateurish. (The fact that so many reviews differ as to what actually happens in the film attests to the dodgy storytelling techniques.)

fluous exposition and talking heads; the fact that much of it was improvised is both a boon and a bane. Whereas the ad-libbed dialogue occasionally adds a level of realism not found in staged fare, some of the monologues are awkward and mar what are otherwise intelligent and interesting characters. Furthermore, many scenes are dragged out much longer than is necessary—the exuberant goings on within a Baptist church being the most burdensome—and smack of padding, even though it's obvious that length wasn't an issue with the director.

Aside from vision, the film has a great deal of merit, although it may take repeated viewings to glean all of it. In addition to being thought provoking and subversive, the script is refreshingly original for the time; to my knowledge it is the first film to use vampirism as a metaphor for drug addiction. (Not once is the word vampire uttered, however, even though it is quickly assumed that the disease is the genesis for the more popularized, traditional bloodsuckers.) *Ganja and Hess* also makes good use of juxtaposing western European iconography with traditional African music and imagery, which in addition to being evocative gives it a cultural and historical context sorely missing in many black films of the time.

DVD box art for Ganja and Hess (1998)
All Day Entertainment #98040001

Technically, *Ganja and Hess* is uneven throughout. Although Hinton's cinematography captures an abundance of arresting images (made even more impressive in that this was shot on Super 16 before being blown up to 35mm for the big screen), it is offset by just as many awkward compositions. A professional looking production in most respects, it is also on occasion hampered by shaky camerawork or grainy footage, possibly a byproduct of the hurried shooting schedule. The cast is composed of both veterans and non actors, and all do surprisingly well in light of the questionable, often awkward, improvisation. The music is one of the film's more consistent attributes, although a gospel number played at the beginning, which reiterates the back story is, well, awkward. Alas, this word of the day best sums up the film's myriad shortcomings.

As far as exploitation, the film bears almost no similarity to the more entertaining fare reviewed in this section. There is some after-the-fact bloodshed, with the gore relegated to a loving close up of Hess sticking a penknife into a prostitute's jugular; the spurting seems a bit watery, but the actual prosthetic used is indistinguishable from real flesh, and consequently disturbing regardless of the consistency of the blood. There is also no shortage of skin, including some full frontal male nudity, something that was rarely seen at the time outside adults only features. Although one would be hard pressed to consider most of it gratuitous, there is a love scene between Ganja and a post nuptial pickup that—like the church sequences—tests the viewer's endurance. The final shot of an unidentified nude man leaping out of a swimming pool and running towards Ganja—one can almost hear the sound of flesh slapping against flesh in his wake—will test viewers in other ways: men, in regards to any anatomically sexual inadequacies they may foster, and women, in regards to any inadequacies their lovers obviously display. Guys, if you watch this film in the presence of the fairer sex, be forewarned that any attempts to fast forward over the final scenes will be met with threats upon one's life and/or manhood.

An Emmy Award winning writer, Gunn (1934–89) only has a few films to his credit as a director, including *Stop!* (1970); unfortunately, this directorial debut was shelved by Warner Brothers and now only exists as a rough cut. His only other genre credit—as an actor—was a role as a police officer in an episode of *The Outer Limits* (1963–65) in 1963. Unfortunately, he passed away of encephalitis (inflammation of the brain) on April 5, 1989, never having had the opportunity to see his film receive a proper release. Duane Jones (1936–88) was of course the star of George A Romero's zombie classic *Night of the Living Dead* (1968). With only a handful of films to his name,

US advertisement herald for Sugar Hill (1974) American International Pictures, Inc.

can scrape up is a cast off pair of slave shackles, circa 1840s, and some moldy dead tissue belonging to one of the attackers. Although the police chief blames stoned hippies for the string of grisly murders, Hill's ex—police lieutenant Valentine (Richard Lawson)—has a hunch about who and what is responsible.

From the opening credit sequence, which has a faux voodoo ceremony overdubbed with the sounds of the Originals' Supernatural Voodoo Woman (available from Motown Records, by the way), one can't mistake this for anything but a seventies voodoo flick. Even though this film still shares ties with such no budget classics as Victor Halperin's *White Zombie* (1932), long gone are the haunting poetry and subtle politics of Jacques Tourneur's *I Walked with a Zombie* (1943). *Sugar Hill* is a single minded shocker that takes *Foxy Brown*'s revenge motif (which it establishes within the first ten minutes of the film), and trades firearms for Haitian curses and the living dead.

As a supernatural horror film, the film barely rates. As a black crime film, the film doesn't fare much better. As a schlock ridden exploitation flick that wallows in its own contrivances, *Sugar Hill* succeeds. Production values are passable, and the performances more than adequate, but the production would have proven far more effective had some care been taken with the horror film staples. The zombies are ultimately ineffectual, especially after a satisfying sequence of the undead rising from their shallow, unmarked graves. With their silver ping pong ball eyes and poorly applied greasepaint, no amount of fake cobwebs will make them scary, machete or no machete. Although some tension can be found during the final confrontation between Morgan and Sugar's undead minions during the last reel, it's too little too late. (The 1974 episode of *Kolchak, the Night Stalker* 'The Zombie' proved far creepier, and that was made for television, for crying out loud.)

The silliest scene, though, is noteworthy for its pure audacity. Every viewer has witnessed someone attacked by a dismembered hand in a horror film; heck, some films, i.e. *The Crawling Hand* (1963), exploit this curious primal fear for all it's worth. If executed properly a scene like this can make for some effective shocks, but to recreate such a scene with a reanimated chicken's foot? Even if you couldn't see the wire awkwardly dragging it around the room, it would be impossible to take very seriously.

Marki Bey is good as Sugar, and although the viewer can't help but picture Grier in the self same role for much of the film, Bey eventually makes the character her own even though she could never hope to measure up. (And, no, I'm not just talking about her cup size, you perverts.) The versatile Lawson plays Miss Hill's concerned ex-hubby Valentine, whose performance is far more subdued than his supporting role in *Scream Blacula Scream* (save for the fact he's sporting a much bigger afro). Quarry—here to fulfill the last of his contractual obligations for AIP—is good, although it's interesting if not a little off-putting to hear him deliver his lines with a southern fried accent. Last but not least, there's Colley, whose enthusiasm in the part of Baron Samedi is… palpable. Although he looks the part, and has the right spirit for the character, he lays on the theatrics (and the eye shadow) a bit too thick. Such a role would require that the actor gnaw on the scenery a bit, to be sure, but it's tough to take the guy seriously when he's camping it up.

And for those that are interested, there is a catfight between Sugar and Morgan's race baiting, cracker moll. Nothing worth shouting about, but scenes like this do keep the proceedings from getting lackadaisical. Also, kudos to the location manager; even though *Sugar Hill* was shot in Houston, Texas, one would have sworn that it was Louisiana. Of course, I've never been to either state, but it's a nice change of pace from the films that assume the viewer can't tell the difference between upstate New York and, say, the jungles of Asia.

One time director Maslansky (1933–) spent most of his last forty years as a producer. He began his career on such low budget (usually imported) horror fare as *Il Castello dei Morti Vivi* [The Castle of the Living Dead] (1964) aka *Crypt of Horror*, *La Sorella di Satana* [The Sister of Satan] (1966) aka *The She-Beast*, and *Death-*

US pressbook advertisement for The Thing With Two Heads (1972) American International Pictures, Inc.

line (1972) aka *Raw Meat*, but eventually made the big time when he began producing the *Police Academy* films in 1984. Writer Kelly (1931–98) only has a couple of films to his credit, including *Cry of the Banshee* (1970). Effects artist Downey supplied the special effects for such wanting killer bug flicks as *Empire of the Ants* and *It Happened at Lakewood Manor* (both 1977). Besides a stint on *Starsky & Hutch* from 1977 to 1979 playing officer Minnie Kaplan, actress Bey (1946–) had a fairly uneventful career. The underrated Quarry (1925–), of course, is most fondly remembered for his contributions to the horror genre in the early seventies, which include both Count Yorga films as well as *The Deathmaster, Dr Phibes Rises Again* (1972) and *Madhouse* (1974). Colley (1938–) also appeared in notable soul cinema *The Legend of Nigger Charley* (1972) and *Black Caesar* (1973).

THE THING WITH TWO HEADS (1972)

American International Pictures, Inc. [US] Saber Productions [US] DIR: Robert Lee Frost (aka Lee Frost) PRO: Wes Bishop SCR: Wes Bishop, Robert Lee Frost (aka Lee Frost) and James Gordon White DOP: Jack Steely EXP: John Lawrence SFX: Rick Baker, Gail Brown, Thomas R Burman, Pete Peterson, Charles H Scram, Daniel C Striepeke and James Gordon White MUS: David Angel, Porter Jordan, Robert O Ragland and Various Artists STR: Rick Baker, Kathryn Baumann, Wes Bishop, John Bliss, Chelsea Brown, Jerry Butler, George C Carey, Tommy Cook, John Dullaghan, Robert Lee Frost (aka Lee Frost), Roger Gentry, Roosevelt Grier (aka Rosey Grier), Phil Hoover, Jane Kellem, Bruce Kimball, Don Marshall, Raymond Milland, Britt Nilsson, Roger Perry, William Smith, Rod Steele, Michael Viner, Dick Whittington and Albert Zugsmith
AKA: *The Beast with Two Heads*
        The Man with Two Heads

Approximately 91m; Color; Rated PG
DVD: *The Thing with Two Heads* [MGM Home
Entertainment; 91m; WS; NTSC R1; Double billed
with The Incredible 2-Headed Transplant]
VHS: *The Thing with Two Heads* [Astral Video;
91m; FS; NTSC]
ADL: "They Transplanted a White Bigot's Head on
a Soul Brother's Body!"

SUFFERING FROM an arthritic condition that
has left him debilitated and wheelchair bound,
wealthy surgeon Dr Maxwell Kirshner (Raymond Milland) is then diagnosed with a pesky
case of terminal chest cancer. He dumps his fortunes into research towards a possible cure: an
experimental procedure that will have his head
grafted onto the body of a living recipient. Once
the body has adapted to the new head, the doctors will then remove the donor's superfluous
noodle, which of course means bad news for the
benefactor. A successful test is had with a gorilla,
although the two-headed ape manages to break
free before the procedure is finished, giving the
confused beast enough time to wreak havoc in a
local grocery store. Convinced it will work on a
human, the doctor's hired hands begin searching
high and low for a suitable donor, but soon find
themselves slumming it when they are forced to
make the offer to inmates on death row.

As it turns out, the dying tycoon is something
of a racist—he fights tooth and nail to break a
contract with a new doctor at his hospital because
the man is a few shades too mocha for his taste—
so it's of little surprise to the viewer that the only
willing person who fits the bill sports a much
darker tan than what the surgeon had in mind.
Innocently charged convict Jack Moss (Rosey
Grier) agrees to the hush-hush procedure in order to give his girlfriend an extra thirty days to
clear his name; the dying surgeon is unconscious
and on life support when the decision is made.
Suffice to say, the convicted felon is none too

pleased when he wakes up and finds himself rub-
bing cheeks with the cracker surgeon; he hightails
it, the police hot on his trail, with another doctor
in tow. ("How 'bout you taking old happy face off
me here," he asks the practicing surgeon, hoping
to be rid of his newfound growth.)

Not a black exploitation film in the strictest
sense (only a few of the cast members are actually black, and it was obviously intended for a
more general drive-in market), *The Thing with
Two Heads* should be included because of the
racially driven script. Sure, the handling of the
material is quite blunt—it rarely rises above such
simplistic Hulk-like truisms as "bigotry bad" and
"don't judge a book by cover"—but it does seem
sincere, which isn't always the case with racially
motivated exploitation films helmed primarily by
white directors. The material also benefits from
the fact that the scriptwriters strive to avoid politically correct two dimensional stereotypes; the
good casting only reinforces them.

The Thing with Two Heads is played primarily
straight for the first reel; once Grier and Milland
start butting heads, the serious issues that were
being tackled early on are cast aside for situation-
al comedy. Unlike many films that attempt to mix
monsters and mirth, this sucker is actually quite
funny when it chooses to be. The extended scene
with a post surgery Grier attempting to escape
from the makeshift laboratory, Milland's gaping,
snoring head hanging limply from his shoulder,
is as funny as anything Monty Python ever conceived. When the reluctant two-headed man first
confronts Grier's girlfriend, the first words out of
her mouth are, "You get into more shit!"

Technically, the film is quite slick, save for
some mildly disorientating zooms. (Not quite as
headache inducing as those perpetrated by the
prolific Jess Franco in his heyday, but obtrusive
nonetheless.) The special effects are passable—
having had a year to improve upon the cine-

Outside of a few silly gadgets, Jesse James Meets Frankenstein's Daughter looks fairly slick despite its threadbare budget. Where was it filmed, and for how much? How did the limited budget affect the production?

The film was shot on location in the San Fernando Valley, for how much I don't know. Other than whom they had as actors—a bigger budget might have bagged better known stars—it had little affect.

How did you get started in acting?

I was working for the Los Angeles Police Department, and I stopped a talent agent for speeding and gave him a ticket. He was impressed with my size and asked me if I ever considered an acting career. I said, "No, not really, but I'm willing to give anything a shot," and pretty soon he was sending me on interviews.

What was that experience like working on the cult television series Star Trek, where you played the part of Keel in the Friday's Child episode? [Airdate December 1, 1967.]

The experience was great, but that was before the show had much of a cult following.

What was your favorite role as an actor, and why?

The role of Arnie in the *Bonanza* episode The Ape, mostly because the director and all of the actors were very easy to work with.

As an actor, what was your greatest regret?

In 1964, a film agent asked me to go to Italy to shoot a string of western movies. I was doing fairly well with the agent I had; I had already done four or five things, including a couple of leading roles. I hated to just go to my agent and say "I'm leaving town," so I decided, "No, I think this guy is doing me all right" and stuck with him. And so

Clint Eastwood was offered the chance to go over there, and… you know the rest of the story.

Why did you give up your acting career in 1968?

It's difficult to hold down a regular job to support your family and still get time off to do a movie. I never worked steady enough to support my family with movie work alone.

Having read an interview with you in The Wenatchee World, it came to my attention that you are a writer of crime fiction. What have you had published so far? What do you currently have in the works?

I wrote a suspense thriller called *Last Reunion*, which was published (as a print on demand book) through www.iuniverse.com. I am currently about 300 pages into my second novel, *Swift Justice*.

What do you think about the thinning line between crime fiction and more outright horror literature, with books like Thomas Harris' The Silence of the Lambs? What authors have influenced your writing the most?

I prefer the suspense genre where the reader is always skirting trouble. Patricia Cornwell and Tami Hoag are two of my favorite writers.

In closing, what do you want the epitaph on your tombstone to read?

Family always came first.

US pressbook advertisement for The Crater Lake Monster (1977) Crown International Pictures

JOHN STANLEY'S NIGHTMARE IN BLOOD

*Interview conducted via email
July 2005*

MOST HORROR fans recognize John Stanley as the author of *The Creature Feature Movie Guide* [Creatures at Large Press; 1981], which remains in print to this day, having been revised and updated no less than five times. Dubbed "the Leonard Maltin of horror films" by the press, Stanley has a reputation that precedes him. Until recently though, many people were unaware that the revered horror film host turned film reviewer had also tried his hand at filmmaking, producing a formidable low budget shocker in the mid seventies called *Nightmare in Blood*. Thanks to the DVD revolution, this is changing.

In 1960, Stanley was hired as a copy boy by *The San Francisco Chronicle*, eventually working his way up to the more prestigious positions of writer and editor on the newspaper's Sunday Datebook stories. Although he devoted much of his spare time to film and book projects throughout the years, he remained on staff at *The San Francisco Chronicles* until his retirement in 1993.

Stanley hooked up with Kenn Davis—a coworker at the *Chronicles* who was also a devout film buff—and in 1970 they decided to try their hand at scriptwriting, producing a screenplay for a film called *The Dark Side of the Hunt*. Much like the 1971 blockbuster *Shaft*, their proposed script featured a black private eye, but this was before the later film helped usher in the black film explosion of the seventies. Unfortunately, Stanley and Davis turned down a modest offer from American International Pictures, as they were instead hoping to produce the film themselves, but they ultimately failed to raise the financing. Still itching to get into filmmaking, the determined duo started work on a second project, which would eventually become *Nightmare in Blood*, a film that—in terms of production—lived up to the nightmare in its title. The film was finally released in 1978 to little fanfare, had a brief run on video in the mid eighties, and then for all intents and purposes was lost, forgotten by everyone except hardcore trashfiends and enthusiasts of obscure horror fare.

With *Nightmare in Blood* in the can but still awaiting distribution, Stanley had two books published, namely *World War III* [Avon Books; 1976] and *The Dark Side* [Avon Books; 1976]. The latter—co-authored by Davis—was based on their unrealized screenplay, and was nominated for the prestigious Edgar Award. Later, Stanley published the Robert Bloch collection *Lost in Time and Space with Lefty Feep* [Creatures at Large Press; 1987] and edited the biography *Them Ornery Mitchum Boys: The Adventures of Robert & John Mitchum* [Creatures at Large Press; 1989].

In 1979, Stanley took over as host for the Saturday night horror program *Creature Features*. First aired in 1971 on KTVU-TV in San Francisco, California, and later on KXTL-TV in Sacramento, host Bob Wilkins would forgo the time honored traditions of greasepaint and scenery chewing, and instead open the shows in

Promotional still of John Stanley on the set of
Creature Features (1979-1984) KXTL-TV

I seem to be in the minority when it comes to rec-
ognizing the merits of the underrated *Nightmare
in Blood*, I hope that my interview and review will
introduce the film to others who will be able to
appreciate it for the self same reasons.

TRASHFIEND: *What was the first horror film
you saw as a child? What kind of impression did
it leave on you?*

JOHN STANLEY: Howard Hawks' *The Thing
from Another World* (1951) was my introduction to movie horror. I spent the entire summer
of '51 afraid to walk down corridors alone, im-
agining that the 'vegetable' creature would leap
out and grab me. And I never forgot the music. I
still think that it's the scariest score—by Dimitri
Tiomkin—ever written for a film. A few months
later *The Day the Earth Stood Still* (1951) reinforced my newfound belief that movies could
be terrifying. I still marvel at how Robert Wise
directed Patricia Neal to respond so realistically
to Gort when he meets her in the park and then
carries her unconscious body into the spaceship.
Her fear when she wakes up alone and trapped in
the ship with Gort is a classic moment.

*As an avid horror fan, what do you see as the
most noticeable differences between modern day
horror films and those of the seventies when
Nightmare in Blood was made? Did you notice
much of a change in trends within the genre from
the moment of its inception in 1972 to its release
in 1978, and do you think that this had an
impact on how the film was received?*

We're all supposed to be so insightful and eru-
dite to notice trends when we're trying to get a
film financed and shot with a minimal crew and
budget? Yeah, sure. Who was worried about other
movies? Or the subtleties of their content? Hardly.
We spent years just trying to get the damn thing

a more leisurely, down to earth fashion, a trade-
mark that Stanley would adopt as well during his
stay, which ended when the show was cancelled
in 1984. Aside from making the occasional cameo in low budget films, Stanley has shied away
from filmmaking and focused on his writing in
the years since.

Having viewed for the first time the nearly forgotten *Nightmare in Blood* only a few years ago, I
was both pleased and surprised to hear Image Entertainment's announcement that they would be
giving a proper release to said film. Being a fan, I
wasted no time in, first, securing a copy of the disc
and, second, tracking down Mr Stanley for an interview, to which he graciously said yes. Although

weighty affair that—if not watched in the wee hours of the morning—is best experienced immediately following any dental appointment that involves Novocain. (Although styles differ drastically, the end results are not unlike those of Andy Milligan's lurid Victorian efforts.) The film overcomes some of its shortcomings through sheer determination, but it is ultimately dragged down by the cumbersome performances and stilted dialogue, Boyette's narration withstanding.

The worst onscreen culprit is our dull and ineffectual hero as portrayed by Harvey, whose application of the dramatic pause is enough to make William Shatner wince, and whose inability to emote borders on catatonic. When asked his thoughts about *Dungeon of Harrow*, Boyette has often attributed some of the films failing to the poor—albeit predetermined—casting of his leading man. It should come as no surprise to anyone who has witnessed his talents that the only reason Harvey produced the film was because he wanted to be in front of the camera. Having endured his performance in *Dungeon of Harrow*, I can comfortably say that the only way he could fulfill his calling as an actor was to pay someone off as he did here. (He bribed Boyette in a similar fashion two years later with *No Man's Land*, which proved to be their last collaboration.)

To make things worse, this character rightly deserves whatever insidious fate befalls him. When confronted with the disappearance of his shipmate, a trail of blood in the missing man's wake, our hero seems barely perturbed and quickly gives up his search for a moonlit stroll with the resident nurse. When the wounded captain attempts to save his comrade by throwing himself into a life and death struggle with de Sade's indentured servant, our oh-so-intrepid hero stands by dumbly and watches his friend get skewered. But when the Count's leprous wife steals a kiss from Aaron, our hero begins screaming like a

DVD box art for Dungeon of Harrow (2002)
Alpha Video Distributors, Inc. #4084-D

frightened schoolgirl, his hair turning white from the traumatic shock.

As if to offer a counter balance, the Count as portrayed by McNulty chews the scenery with as much gusto as any cut rate thespian could muster for minimum wage and his name up in lights. The character's turgid struggle with his bedeviled id results in perturbing hallucinations, including a manifestation of his own darker half, "a product of his evil, a reflection of his madness", that taunts him for a few moments before dropping a giant laugh-out-loud spider in his lap. (It doesn't seem like it should be much of a struggle for the old chap by this point, as he's obviously been quite open in the expression of his sadistic tendencies for years with little or no remorse.)

The other actors aren't nearly as polar in their extremes, although the only face with any real talent and/or experience is Morgan (1902–67),

Mexican lobby card for Dungeon of Harrow (1962) Distribuidora Rivero

who plays the fairly likeable captain. As an actor (often uncredited), Morgan had appeared in over forty films since 1943, most of those westerns. (He also showed up in Boyette's sexy sci fi flick *The Weird Ones* the same year.) On the flip side, Harris is thankfully given only a handful of lines. It is probably safe to assume that, as a basketball player for one of the Harlem Globetrotters' subsidiary teams, he was much more adept on court than he was on stage. One might think Harvey only gave Harris a part so that *he* could upstage at least one of the other cast members. It almost worked.

The contrived script displays little originality, but remains somewhat engaging *because* it combines so many different elements. Of course, this necessitates that the narrative sacrifice logic for convenience. Once the character of Ann is no

longer of any use to the script, she dies from a Chinese water torture session having been subjected to it for less than twenty four hours. Later, the Count's manservant is rudely discarded simply because he wants to take a breather during the 'climactic' chase scene, making it feasible for Aaron to take out de Sade on his own. (And God knows our hero needs all the help he can get.)

The viewer may get the impression that they are watching a live action comic book—no surprise considering the man in charge of the production. Not only is the stilted dialogue more suited for the printed page—one can almost see the word balloons floating about the heads of the players—many a scene is even framed like a comic panel, with the camera only moving when absolutely necessary. So much does it feel like a piece one would find buried in the pages of Scary

The lovely Miss Steele and friend huddle in terror at the presence of an orthodontically-challenged ghost in the sequel to Riccardo Freda's Euro-gothic classic, *L'Orrible Segreto del Dr. Hichcock: L'Orrible Segreto del Dr. Hichcock*. Belgian window card for *Lo Spettro* (1963) Stellor Films

A Spanish B-movie heroine is shocked and appalled at the cheap plastic Halloween teeth sported by prolific co-star Paul Naschy. I wonder if his pair came with a whistle. Belgian window card for *La Marca del Hombre-Lobo* (1968) Maxper Producciones Cinematograficas

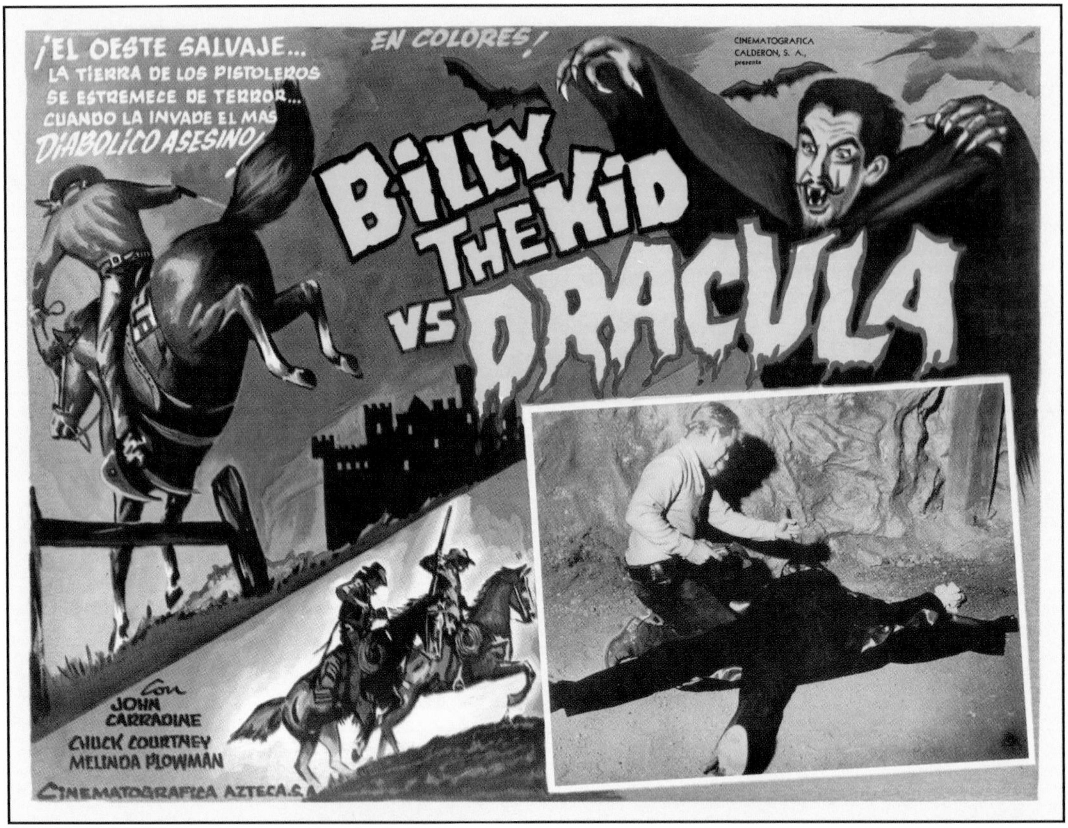
¡EL OESTE SALVAJE...
LA TIERRA DE LOS PISTOLEROS
SE ESTREMECE DE TERROR...
CUANDO LA INVADE EL MAS
DIABOLICO ASESINO!
EN COLORES!
CINEMATOGRAFICA
CALDERON, S. A.,
presenta
BILLY THE KID VS DRACULA
Con
JOHN
CARRADINE
CHUCK COURTNEY
MELINDA PLOWMAN
CINEMATOGRAFICA AZTECA

1

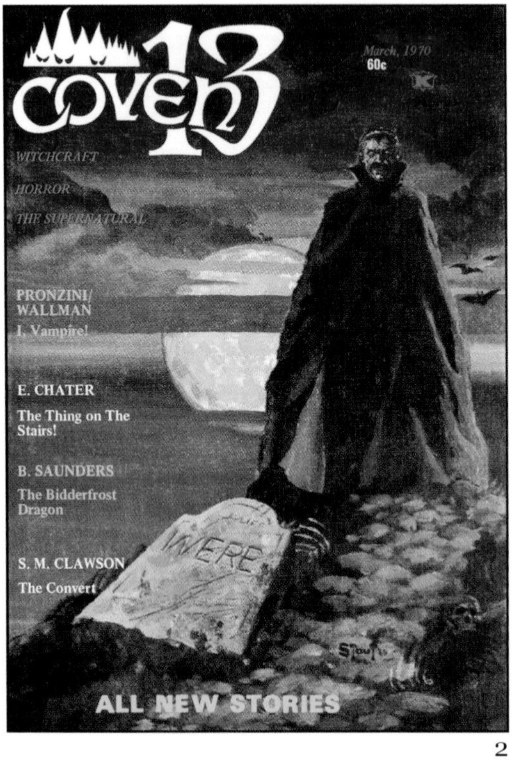
COVEN 13
March, 1970
60c
WITCHCRAFT
HORROR
THE SUPERNATURAL
PRONZINI/
WALLMAN
I, Vampire!
E. CHATER
The Thing on The
Stairs!
B. SAUNDERS
The Bidderfrost
Dragon
S. M. CLAWSON
The Convert
ALL NEW STORIES

2

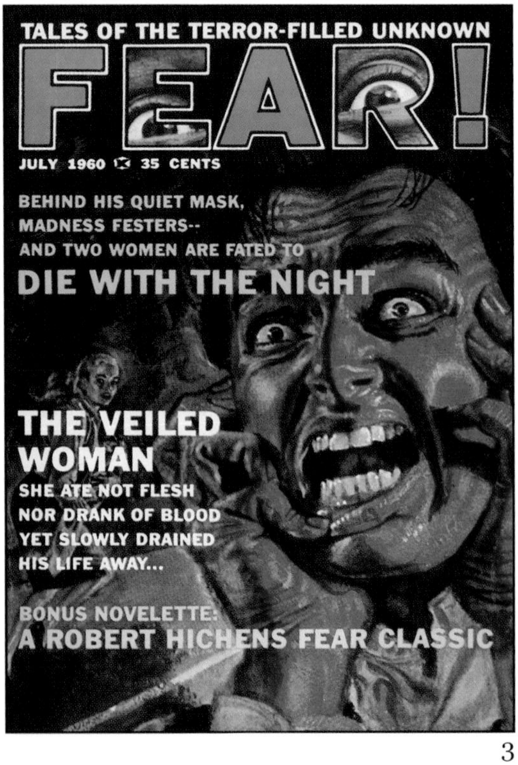
TALES OF THE TERROR-FILLED UNKNOWN
FEAR!
JULY 1960 35 CENTS
BEHIND HIS QUIET MASK,
MADNESS FESTERS--
AND TWO WOMEN ARE FATED TO
DIE WITH THE NIGHT
THE VEILED
WOMAN
SHE ATE NOT FLESH
NOR DRANK OF BLOOD
YET SLOWLY DRAINED
HIS LIFE AWAY...
BONUS NOVELETTE:
A ROBERT HICHENS FEAR CLASSIC

3

1

2

3

Previous page [**1**] The notorious, apparently misunderstood outlaw stakes the enfeebled bloodsucker shortly after knocking him for a loop with a thrown firearm. And who says guns have no effects on vampires? Mexican lobby card for *Billy the Kid vs. Dracula* (1965) Cinematografica Azteca, S.A. [**2**] Dracula ponders the cryptic epitaph of "Were" on a fallen tombstone, unaware that someone with no sense of humor has scratched out the preceding "You" and succeeding "Here." Cover art by William Stout for *Coven 13* v1#4 (March 1970) Camelot Publishing Company [**3**] If that's his "quiet mask," how'd he secure one date, let alone two? I guess beggars can't be choosers when you go with one of them online dating services. Cover art by GAP for *Fear!* v1#2 (July 1960) Great American Publications, Inc.

This page [**1**] I've heard ballet instructors can be real monsters, but this seems like a pretty extreme method for teaching an aspiring student en second lieu position des bras. Cover art for the 8mm excerpt from *L'Amante del Vampiro* (1960) Ken Films #2217 [**2**] Cover art for the 8mm excerpt from *The Mummy's Ghost* (1944) Castle Films #1049 [**3**] *The Claw Monsters*. Although uncredited, the artwork for this reel looks suspiciously like that of Wallace Wood. Cover art for the 8mm excerpt from *Panther Girl Of The Kongo* (1955) United Arista #HA-5 [**4**] If you asked me, the Count looks a little too jovial having a big hunk of splintered wood sticking out of his sternum. But then again, it looks more like a chocolate ice cream cone than a wooden stake, so maybe things aren't as dire as one would think. Box art for *Creepy Creatures: Dracula Jigsaw Puzzle* (1975) H-G Toys, Inc. #455-02

Woweeee!!.........that's what I call a **DRY** MARTINI !!!!

SOFT CAPTIVE OF TERROR **MOUNTAIN**
By BRUCE CHANDLER

SHOCK

A LOVELY BRIDE
FOR SATAN
By ANDREW BLAKE

OCT.
k 35¢

MY____ TALES

HORROR'S
HANDMAIDENS
By BILL RYDER

DREADNIGHT
By JAMES ROSENQUEST

TEMPTRESS FROM THE BLACK PIT
By ART CROCKETT

[1] If you ever wondered from whence I get my sophisticated sense of humor (a ponderance which I'm certain has haunted you many a long, sleepless night), then look no further than a certain Seattle horror host. An evocative still of Joe "The Count" Towey from the late night horror program *Nightmare Theatre* (circa 1970s) KIRO-TV

[2] C'mon, people, this is funny stuff! Oh, well, as per usual, the author stands alone… Header design for *Monsters, Ghouls & Assorted Creeps Stationary Pad* (1965) Paula #ASP-108

[3] Nobody expects the Spanish Inquisition! Well, apparently this particular soft captive isn't terribly surprised or perturbed by their unannounced visit to Terror Mountain. I guess she got the memo… Cover art for *Shock Mystery Tales* v2#5 (October 1962) Pontiac Publishing Corp.

the original negative for the film was allowed to deteriorate through sheer neglect), *Mad Monster Party?* holds up extremely well, even against their more universally loved films. One of their earliest claymation efforts, *Mad Monster Party?* is very 'cinematic,' more so than most of their productions. The cinematography is comparatively epic, having avoided the claustrophobic but homey feel Animagic films usually evoke, and is visually impressive despite the occasionally clunky animation.

Maury Laws' music isn't nearly as infectious as that found in the Christmas specials, although one number, Stay One Step Ahead, would make a perfect companion piece to One Foot In Front Of The Other from *Santa Claus is Coming to Town.* Fans of sixties trash horror will appreciate the music far more than the average Rankin and Bass fan, as it evokes the themes that could be found punctuating such shows as *The Munsters* (1964–66) and *The Ghost and Mr Chicken* (1966). Furthermore, the partygoers are treated to the sounds of Little Tibia and the Phibbeans, a long haired group of skeletons that play generic mid sixties psychedelic garage rock that wouldn't sound terribly out of place performed by the Saturday morning cartoon outfit The Groovie Goolies.

Even though the clichéd jokes have a certain dated charm about them, one may quickly tire of the groan inducing one-liners and drawn out sight gags (particularly in the case of one sequence that has the monsters either sleeping off the bash, or trying to deal with their brethren's snoring). Similarities to *Mad* magazine are quite apropos, when one discovers it was written by Harvey Kurtzman, one of EC's premier humor writers. There are rumors that Forrest J Ackerman (1916–2008) of *Famous Monsters of Filmland* fame, was an uncredited co-writer on the film, but they have not been substantiated. (If it is true, we could probably attribute, nay, *blame* many of the painful wordplays on him;

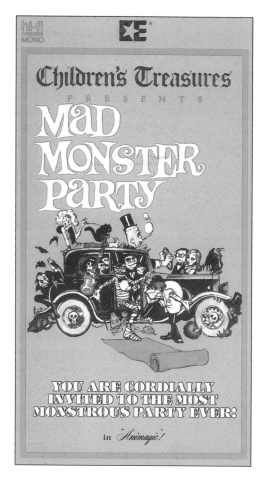

VHS box art for Mad Monster Party? (1985)
Embassy Home Entertainment #2077

anyone raised on the seminal monster magazine will cringe at remembrances of the editor's more excruciating puns. Forry, we love you dearly and hold you in the highest regard, and always will, but some things should just be illegal.) Some of the best jokes involve Yetch's unrequited love for the seemingly frigid Francesca, and it is disappointing that tired slapstick is often favored over more inspired scenes like this.

Much of the film's strength lies in the amazing designs by comic artist Jack Davis, another EC veteran and *Mad* contributor. Davis' comic interpretations of the classic film monsters are amus-

Like a deer caught in Francesca's headlights, Yetch professes
his profound love for the busty redhead.
Still from Mad Monster Party? (1967)
Embassy Pictures Corp./Videocraft International

ing whilst retaining a certain dignity usually lost in such spoofs; this talent is what made much of his work for *Mad* so timeless. Furthermore, his distinct style makes a successful transition from the drawing board to film, as the animators had the smarts and sensibility to remain true to his designs as much as possible.

Complementing the designs are the gifted vocal actors. Karloff's presence grounds the film in classic monster cinema like no one else could. (He had previously worked with Rankin and Bass as a voice actor on their first collaboration with producer Levine, *The Daydreamers*.) Unfortunately, the ailing, crippled actor would pass away a few years later having appeared in a handful of Mexican low budget horror flicks. Stand up comedian Diller gives the film a certain edge as well, offering a counterbalance to Karloff's more subtle deliveries. (As a running gag in her comedy routines, Diller often refers to her fictional husband as Fang; whether or not this joke preceded *Mad Monster Party?* or was instead inspired by it,

I do not know.) Animagic mainstay Allen Swift supplies voices for most of the other monsters; he does a fairly admirable job emulating the late Peter Lorre (1904–64) in his portrayal of Frankenstein's kickboy Yetch. Last but not least are Ethel Ennis (1932–) and Gale Garnett (1942–), the latter of whom was an RCA Victor recording artist with the oft covered top forty hit We'll Sing In The Sunshine to her credit.

Another facet that makes *Mad Monster Party?* interesting is that, despite being a film aimed at a younger audience, it boasts not only a fair number of sexual innuendos, but also displays some coy yet pervasive sexism. The heroine, Francesca, is a strong willed and ruthless (read: frigid) woman who eventually thaws and falls head over heels for her sworn nemesis after he gallantly rescues her. (Their love is apparently cinched after Felix slaps her around in order to quell her hysteria. Now if that isn't old world sexual politics, I don't know what is.) Of course, had the film been made today, Francesca wouldn't be sporting such tremendous headlights (even though it would be more realistic in light of our country's rampant silicone abuse), and the catfight scene between her and the monster's mate (dubbed over with the sounds of real cats going at it tooth and nail) would probably be handled with a little more tact.

Originally tagged with the working title *The Monster Movie*, it was later changed to include the word 'mad' to cash in on Davis and Kurtzman's association with the magazine of the same name, according to Animagic historian Rick Goldschmidt in his book *The Enchanted World of Rankin & Bass* [Tiger Mountain Press, 1997]. Included in the same book is the original one-sheet poster art proposed by Jack Davis, which—instead of having the title replaced and the art recycled—was simply scrapped. (Also featured are Davis' original character designs and numerous behind the scenes photos.) On the same note, noted fantasy artist

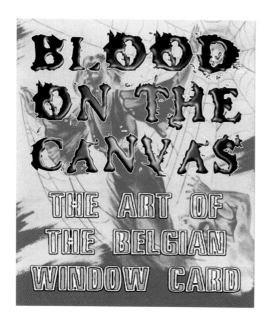

BLOOD ON THE CANVAS: THE ART OF THE BELGIAN WINDOW CARD

TUCKED BETWEEN France, Germany and the Netherlands and bordering the North Sea, Belgium is one of the smallest countries in Europe; covering nearly 12,000 square miles, it is barely larger than the state of Maryland in the United States. A thickly populated country, it is only natural that film has been an extremely popular pastime since it was introduced. Belgium has it own film industry, but being a small country of limited means has depended a great deal on imports to fill the slots on marquees.

As favored in most European countries during the sixties and seventies, many of these imports were exploitation films, as the distribution rights could be had reasonably cheap. The posters used to promote these films were stylistically not unlike those issued by other European countries. By the early seventies, nudity and gore was often quite prominent for more gratuitous cinematic offerings. Atypical to form, the most lurid pieces were sometimes the most beautifully rendered as well.

Eschewing photos for painted artwork (although a touched up still is incorporated into the artwork on occasion), most of these posters offer colorful acrylic and oil based renderings of scenes from the films, with the occasional tempera wash thrown in for variety. During the first half of the seventies, there was a trend among artists producing Belgian posters for genre films—primarily horror and sexploitation—to work in the medium of brush and black ink. Almost indistinguishable from what one could find in European comic books at the time, the posters offered some zest by highlighting the b&w illustrations with large red fills.

The window cards produced in Belgium were 14" wide by 2" tall, with a 2" to 3" empty band across the top so theatres could write in play dates and/or show times. They resembled American window cards, except that the American equivalent was 14" x 22" and printed on heavy cardstock. Cards from Belgium were generally printed on thinner one-sheet stock, matt for most titles released prior to 1970, and a glossy finish for most released thereafter.

What also sets Belgian cards apart is that the titles for the release are given in both French and Flemish, the two official languages of the country. Occasionally, the original title is listed as well, at least as far as English language titles are concerned. Obviously, this can make easy identification of imports that are otherwise obscured by lack of technical information, especially when the art bears no resemblance to the art used to promote the films in other countries.

In the gallery, I have tried to include a variety of styles that were applied to window cards for horror fare in the sixties and seventies. Unfortunately, much of their grandeur is lost in the b&w reproductions, but it is still easy to see the ways in which Belgian cards differed from their peers. Please note that, in order to reproduce as much of the artwork as possible, I have cropped the area that is usually left blank at the top of some cards.

Belgian window card for Un Bianco Vestito per Marialé (1972) Cosmopolis Films

Bruce Jones' work takes a turn for the Poe-etic in "Clarice," illustrated by Berni Wrightson.
Creepy #77 (February 1976) Warren Publishing

quite well. Some of it, of course, is just dumb luck. My understanding is that the filming conditions on *Chain Saw* were really loathsome and that they were glad to get anything at all on raw stock by the end of the day—or the end of the morning as was often the case. You rarely ever know why a film works while you're shooting it, and you certainly never know what makes a classic. As Brando said, it's always a crapshoot.

What do you consider the pinnacles in horror, whether it be film or literature, and why? What do you consider the low points of the genre?

It's a hard question because the answer is so relative. Poe obviously did great work, but then on the other hand so did Val Lewton. These things really boil down to personal taste, which is rarely based on anything easily described or nec-

essarily analytical. What Robert Ebert used to call guilty pleasures. Films and books that make a major impression on us—like *The Creeper*—don't always have a great deal of aesthetic merit. They just ring our bell for some reason, probably by touching some nerve in our personal psyche, usually during our youth. You guys are into the seventies stuff because it made an impact on your formative years. Most of my formative film years were spent watching b&w movies because that's all TV was, and a large number of theatrical films were still being made in b&w back then. To me it always had a dreamlike, graphic quality color never seemed to attain. But I can't get my own kid to even watch b&w films because they weren't in flux with his system. So it's all relative. The trouble with color genre films for me is that you're always looking at the color, which can become a

Veal, anyone? A panel from the splash page of Bruce Jones' "As Ye Sow," illustrated by Luis Bermejo.
Creepy #79 (May 1976) Warren Publishing

distraction in itself. B&w is subtler. The blacks are true blacks and a counterpoint to the whites. You have only two elements making up the matrix that forms the images.

What comic books influenced you most as a child?

I read *Tarzan* and *Mighty Mouse* because that's what was around. I didn't come into regular comic reading until after the Code, so I had to pick up the EC and other horror and sci fi titles at used bookstores during college. But back then there were so many more companies publishing comics, such a wide variety of attitude to choose from. Very eclectic, which is usually a good thing, though we had our share of money grubbing sharks shoveling out their tripe. When I was a kid, all kids read comic books. There was no such thing as a nerd, or an elitist if you will. Comics were a big part of popular culture and, like the movies, another place to find color narrative. But it certainly wasn't hip. I never let my girlfriends know I read them. That would have been death. The movies and graphic novels helped change all that.

Your work as an illustrator was very stylized and very distinct, and fondly remembered by horror

fans of my generation who grew up on Warren and Skywald. When did you decide that you wanted to become a comic artist or writer? Who were your biggest influences? Why was it you abandoned illustration in the mid seventies and solely pursued a writing career?

I decided to study art in college and pursue it as a career in New York because it seemed the path of least resistance. I was the kid who could always outdraw the other kids in class, you know. My influences were Hal Foster, Frazetta, Williamson, and all those guys with an illustrative style. I was as much in pursuit of commercial art gigs as I was with comics, but the comic work just seemed to become more regular. I was never a fast artist, though, and you must retain a certain speed in this business to stay above water. So I eventually segued into writing pretty much full time. With drawing you're chained to a board all day and night… writing lets you walk around the mall while you're thinking about the plot. I guess I'm gregarious by nature. I like to watch people.

I didn't actually withdraw totally from drawing; I just took on less work in that field so I could spend more time at it, using writing to pay the bills. Looking back, I wish I'd spent even more time at it. I think I had the potential to do some first class work but much of it looks rushed now. I was always punished by the deadlines. This is, after all, a business before an art.

Would you ever consider getting back into illustrating, or do you feel this part of your comics work is behind you?

I never was one to plan very far ahead with my life. The best drawing like the best writing is done because you want to, not because you're being paid for it. But once marriage and children become a part of your life you have to take a more philosophical approach to what you're doing. I've been thinking about doing some painting recently but not in the sequential storytelling mold. Just stuff I'd like to do for my own pleasure, not necessarily genre related. But I may change my mind. I often do.

Although you toyed around with fantasy and sci fi, most of your work from the seventies was horror. Was this a conscious decision, a preference, or was it more a matter of supply and demand, since much of your work was with publishers like Warren who were devoted to the genre?

A little of each, but mostly probably supply and demand. You go where the work is. I always considered myself a writer first, then worried about the genre later. I was not as successful as a superhero writer or mystery novelist as I was as a horror writer so I stuck with what I was making a living at. I always thought my best work was in my novels. But in the end, you're only as good as whatever editor is buying your stuff. I just seemed to have better luck with comic book editors than novel editors or TV and movie producers, though I had my share of incredibly inept comic editors. I always wonder how much really great stuff is out there hidden in the drawers of writers and artists all over the country simply because some editor

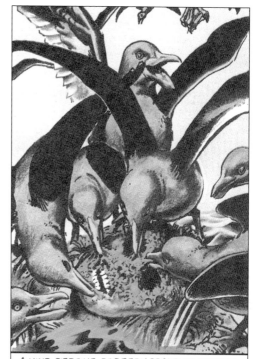

A MIND-PIERCING *SCREECH* BROKE HIS REVERIE. HE *JOLTED* UP, EYES FIXING CONFUSEDLY ON HIS WIFE'S CORPSE...AS IF *SHE* MIGHT SUPPLY ANSWERS. HIS STOMACH *TWISTED*. HER FACE WAS HALF *GONE*. THE SKY WAS *FILLED* WITH GULLS...

Richard Corben illustrates Bruce Jones' "In Deep."
Creepy #83 (October 1976) Warren Publishing

didn't have the foresight to recognize what he had in front of him. It's a tough business, and sometimes a disheartening one. But every so often very, very rewarding as well.

How did you meet Jeff Jones, with whom you share many similarities artistically? It appears that, as friends and peers, you may have had some influence over each other's approach to illustration.

Jeff was one of the first people I met when I first came to New York. I think I was taking samples of my stuff to the Warren offices back then and they weren't interested but suggested I go see Jeff who was new in town and whose style was reminiscent of mine. I went to see him in his tiny, roach ridden apartment and we hit it off right away. Jeff was the guy I could sit around with for hours and jaw about fine art without once touching on comics. He introduced me to Brangwyn and Cole and other great illustrators and we haunted old bookstores together with Roy Krenkel. And, yes, we shared a fan boy worship of Frazetta and Williamson and used to go up and visit them regularly before they became legends. Everyone was so open, so accessible back then. Not a narcissistic head in the group. It was great. Comics were looked upon with general disdain by the public at large, but we didn't give a damn. We were out to change the world. The brevity of youth, you know?

Some of your best work was with Berni Wrightson, to whom your writing seems very suited, in particular such unforgettable pieces as 'Clarice,' 'Jennifer' and 'The Laughing Man.' How did the collaboration process work? Did you write these stories knowing he was to illustrate them?

Berni and Jeff and Mike Kaluta and I all came to New York at almost exactly the same time—it was sheer coincidence, serendipity really—four guys from completely disparate parts of the country coming together at that precise time with those same general interests. We hung out together and supported each other morally through the tough times. I began working with Berni because Jeff's then wife Louise Jones was editing the Warren line and Berni and I were close friends who admired each other's work. I always knew I was writing a particular story for him. Corben was the same way. We just clicked. It was a fortuitous time.

Some of your earliest professional work was on the sadly short-lived horror comic anthology Web of Horror, which I assume came about due to your association with Jeff Jones and Berni

Wrightson. Your work also appeared in the extremely rare fan produced magazine Abyss #1 (1970). What can you tell us about these publications?

My first published work was actually doing one page [illustrations] for *Amazing* and *Fantastic* sci fi magazines. I think the first comic story of mine was for *Web of Horror*, but I may be wrong. Our little gang of iconoclasts was tired of the routine and lack of imagination up at DC and Marvel during those days and *Abyss* was a result of that. We just wanted to do what we wanted to do the way we wanted to do it. It didn't sell worth a plug nickel, though I think we broke even after printing costs. The guys at Image did it twenty years later and became rich.

Why was Web of Horror cancelled after the third issue? Your contribution for the aborted fourth issue, 'Outside-In,' was later published in the second issue of This is Reality (1971). Was this your only contribution to Web of Horror #4, and if not did the others ever see print?

Web of Horror was published by a guy named Robert Sproul who also published *Cracked* magazine. He was trying to cash in on the Warren horror books. Sci fi writer Terry Bisson was the editor. When Bisson quit after issue three, Berni and I took over as co-editors. We worked very hard putting together some great already completed jobs, throwing out the crappy stuff and putting in some new work of our own. But Sproul had lost interest in the book; apparently it wasn't making enough money to suit him. He strung us along forever with vague promises but nothing ever came to fruition. I went back into the stock room and tried to return all the finished originals to their respective artists, those commissioned by Sproul but never paid. Then Berni and I tossed in the towel. It was a shame. There was some classy stuff in there. Berni did a fourth issue painted cover of a three-armed guy in a swamp holding a knife behind his back that was a knockout. The story inside was called 'One Too Many' and published elsewhere later on, I believe.

In a dedication to Wrightson you wrote in 1977, you mention a collaboration with him called 'The Jade Hand' commissioned by National Periodical Publications aka DC Comics, but never published by them. What can you tell us about this particular piece? Did it ever see print elsewhere?

I don't remember too much about it. I was trying to break into DC at the time without much luck. I think Berni had started the job and grown bored with it and I offered to finish it or something. I don't believe it was ever published. When I think about it now, the idea of marrying my style with Berni's sounds pretty bizarre. Possibly whoever the editor was thought so too.

You had a handful of stories published by Skywald during their short but impressive stint as a purveyor of horror comic magazines. What was it like working for Al Hewetson and his Horror-Mood Team?

Skywald asked me to come on as regular writer and editor of their books after seeing some of my stuff. I thought it was a company desperately in need of editorial guidance. But we couldn't work out a price. Hewetson came along later and they started doing stories with the old Heap character along with a lot of Hewetson's writing. They gave him the job of editor. I think they were having a hard time staying afloat by then and they cut the page rates and ran a lot of so-so material. I pretty much lost interest with what Hewetson was doing with that whole Horror-Mood routine—a phrase that still doesn't make a lot of sense to me. I think Warren was beating the socks off them at a time even Warren was fighting to stay alive. The b&w magazines never made the kind of money

the color comics brought in. After the horror boom of the fifties, and its demise with the Comics Code, superheroes pretty much ruled. Which remains the case today. No one seems to care for the episodic format anymore.

It appears your output during the seventies was predominantly published by Jim Warren, particularly during the latter half of the decade. What was it like working for them? Did you have any control over who illustrated your stories?

I didn't need control because Louise Jones, who edited the books, had great taste and a genuine interest in getting the best art possible, even when the meager budget didn't always allow that. Warren was one of the first publishers to take advantage of the foreign art market, which was cheap to get but still offered some class material. I liked a few of the European artists, but my favorites were still the Wrightsons and Corbens and Heaths. Louise was very gracious about giving my scripts to top notch artists both here and abroad. She was a dream to work for—a very intuitive, very bright woman. She lent a lot to the business and deserves more credit.

Why was your work for Warren fairly sporadic until 1976 when you became a regular contributor, with some issues of Creepy and Eerie featuring as many as three contributions by you?

I had been trying to break into Warren for quite some time as a writer without success. I got a few jobs illustrating other writer's stories but the then editor, Bill Dubay, wasn't keen on my prose. Then I wrote 'Jennifer' and he went ape. He gave it to Berni to illustrate. Shortly after that I moved from New York back to the midwest. About this same time Dubay quit Warren. I then got a call from Louise 'Weezie' Jones telling me she was the new editor and would I like to send in some more scripts? I said sure, and she bought nearly

A particularly brutal but strikingly choreographed page of sequential art by writer/artist Bruce Jones
from the story "Hung Up," published in Nightmare #8 (1972) Skywald Publishing

everything I sent from the very first. It was one of the happiest relationships I ever had with an editor. It didn't hurt, of course, that we were already friends through her husband Jeff. Like any other business, comics are about connections.

Aside from your collaborations with Wrightson, your most memorable work was with underground artist Richard Corben, another illustrator with whom your stories have an affinity despite his and Wrightson's very different styles.

Can we assume that this was also a favorable partnership, since you continued to work with him into the nineties?

Oh, yeah. Rich and I got along great, and he lived just a few miles from me in Kansas City so it was like having Berni or Jeff around in the midwest. We had similar interests at the time and even fooled around with making films together. Again it was just total serendipity, being in the right place at the right time with the right publisher and editor. You can't make those kinds of things happen, they have a will of their own. At the time we took it for granted, it was just work. We had no idea in the least that anyone would actually remember that stuff. We were young and feeling our oats and just hanging out. It was fun and we were making a living.

One of your most memorable collaborations with Corben was the oft reprinted story 'In Deep,' which was both a poignant and truly shocking story of the highest order. What prompted you to write a sequel a couple of years later?

I really don't recall. I remember that 'In Deep' was well received and won me an award I think. Maybe Corb said he was interested in doing a sequel or maybe it was Weezie's idea, I don't know. I remember I was disappointed when Corb didn't do it and the artwork was less than stellar. But then, so was the story, probably. Good rule of thumb: don't attempt to top yourself.

Aside from yourself, what artist do you feel best complemented your horror prose during the seventies? If not Wrightson and/or Corben, are there any other artists during this time that you feel truly did your work justice?

It would have to be Russ Heath. He was a childhood hero of mine so it was an honor working with him. And he did absolutely great things with my scripts. I wish we could have done even

more together. Russ is such a giant talent, truly one of the greats. The only other time I worked with such an amazing pool of artistic talent was on *Twisted Tales* and *Alien Worlds* and that probably wouldn't have happened without the Warren books. My one regret is not being able to get Russ for those books. He was busy with a daily strip at the time.

What horror-oriented story from the seventies are you most proud of, and why?

I really don't have a particular favorite. Wrightson, Corben, Heath—all those guys did great jobs in completely different ways. It's impossible for me to pick a favorite. Some of my best stories went to artists of lesser talent, I remember, so I tend to not recall the stories themselves. But that's the business. You can't always hit the nail on the head. I was very lucky to hit it more than most.

You have been having much success with The Incredible Hulk as of late. Having spent much of your career as an exemplary horror writer, were you eager to try your hand at other genres?

Yeah. I would liked to have moved around in the business a lot more than I did, but you tend to get stereotyped early on and it's hard to shake a label. *Hulk* has been a lot of fun though and I'm happy about its success. It's the kind of book I never dreamed I'd be associated with but I couldn't be more pleased that it's worked out well. The fan response has been nice after all these years, especially coming from a non horror-oriented audience. And it's fun being back in comics again after a long absence. I always considered it as legitimate an art form as any other. And just as hard to do well. Maybe harder.

❏ Bruce Jones: selected horror magazine checklist, see page 282

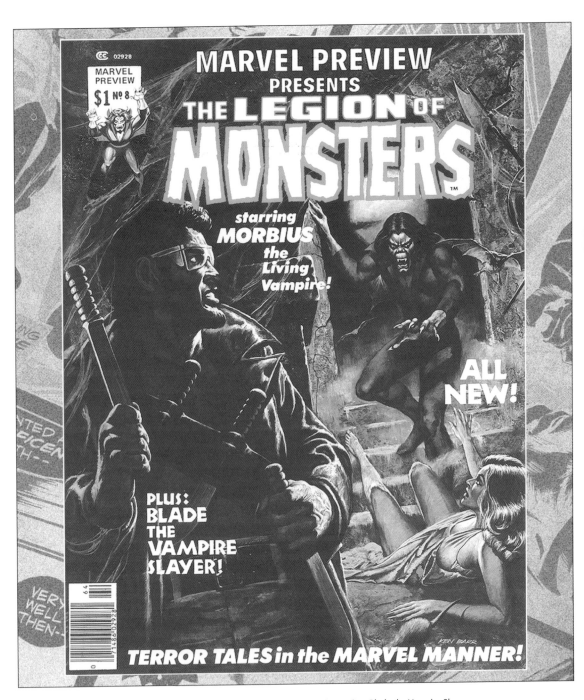

Painter Kenneth Barr pits Morbius the Human Vampire against Blade the Vampire Slayer.

Cover art for Marvel Preview V1#8 (Fall 1976) Marvel Comics Group

Those Marvelous Monsters

A Look at Marvel Comics' Horror Magazines

Lights pinpointing, emphasizing, accentuating his horrible ugliness…freezing on garish scars and stitches of catgut, riveting moldering flesh grey with a queasy pallor no amount of stolen blood could flush with life…stark light hitting his hideously corrupt face with shadows from a shelved brow, drowning creases and deep gouges chiseled from deteriorated flesh ravaged by grave and vermin alike.

Excerpt from 'Frankenstein 1974: The Conscience of the Creature' by Doug Moench, *Monsters Unleashed!* v1#9 (Dec 1974) Marvel Comics Group

WARREN. SKYWALD. EERIE PUBLICATIONS. The names of such publishers evoke a bygone era, a time when horror comics not only flourished as four-color books but also as more mature b&w magazines. From the rise of the format in the sixties, to the glutting of the market in the seventies, to its demise in the early eighties, the format has not been forgotten. Whereas these other companies were primarily magazine publishers, those responsible for 'The World's Greatest Comics' decided to try their hand at the format, creating some endearing contributions to the genre.

Since its groundbreaking namesake was published in 1939 by Timely, Marvel Comics is an entity that has far exceeded the boundaries of the comic book industry. Starting with *Amazing Mysteries* v1#32 (May 1949), Marvel began publishing a number of horror anthologies that survived the Kefauver Senate Hearings and the advent of the puritanical Comics Code Authority. These titles went into hibernation during the sixties when Marvel's distinct approach to superheroes not only spelled a revival for that genre, but also soon dominated the comics market. The demand for more grisly comics fare, though, was far from dead, and became the bread and butter for several smaller publishers who exploited this niche. Sensing there was still a profit to be made from horror fans, but apparently unaware that the market couldn't withstand much more, Marvel took another stab at the genre during the monster craze of the seventies.

Marvel's first foray into publishing a magazine devoted to monsters, in 1964, was a slim fumetti style book called *Monsters to Laugh With* featuring "Filmdom's Funniest Fiends", which—after three issues—changed its name to *Monsters Unlimited*. This short-lived magazine included photos from various creature features accompanied by humorous captions penned by Mr Excelsior

Marvel's first attempt to milk the horror genre.
Amazing Mysteries V1#32 (May 1949) Timely Comics

himself, Stan Lee. Although they were rarely much better than Forrest J Ackerman's puns in *Famous Monsters of Filmland*, these magazines still offered desperate readers a great opportunity to pour over rare film stills from the golden age of movie monsters. Marvel's publication was an aberration, and was more an attempt to cash in on the current trend of funny fiendom represented by the success of television shows like *The Munsters* (1964–66). (Marvel tried to resuscitate this formula with *Monster Madness* in 1972, but it died with the third issue despite the new articles that accompanied the hand me down gags.)

It wasn't until the early seventies that Marvel decided to make the jump into helming an entire line of b&w magazines, having taken an occasional stab at the format in the past. Their first successful magazine publication—in regard to

both returns and fan response—was *Savage Tales* (1971–75). In addition to boasting an early appearance of Robert E Howard's Conan the Barbarian (established as a four-color comic the previous year), the first issue also included the first appearance of the Man-Thing, a character that would become something of a fixture in Marvel's forthcoming horror books. (Over thirty years after making his debut, Artisan Entertainment released *Man-Thing* [2005], an insulting made for cable television misinterpretation of the beloved shambling mound for indiscriminate comic fans and uneducated filmgoers.)

In light of the receptive market, the leading comic company decided to expand its catalogue of oversized, Comics Code Authority exempt titles. Many of these books were horror related and produced by Sal Brodsky (1923–84), who in 1970 had left Marvel to start Skywald Publishing with Herschell Waldman. (Skywald's longest running books, *Nightmare* (1970–75) and *Psycho* (1971–75), were created to cash in on the demand created by Jim Warren's successful line of b&w horror magazines.) Having received an offer he couldn't refuse, Brodsky handed over Skywald's reins to Alan Hewetson in 1972 and returned to Marvel in order to oversee their new line of creature comics. It is not surprising that these early Marvel horror magazines bear some similarities to the Skywald efforts Brodsky had left behind.

Initially, Marvel's horror comic magazines adhered to a formula: one third new material, usually featuring characters intended for serialized adventures; one third articles devoted to the magazine's titular subject, usually as perceived in film and folklore; and one third golden age comic reprints from Marvel's archives by such prolific artists and writers as Tony di Preta, Bernard Krigstein and Paul Reinman. (Most of the recycled material was culled from such juvenile delinquent inspiring ti-

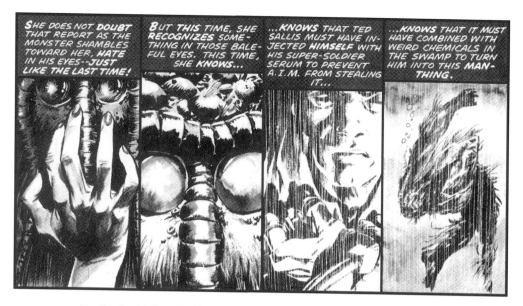

SHE DOES NOT **DOUBT** THAT REPORT AS THE MONSTER SHAMBLES TOWARD HER, **HATE** IN HIS EYES—**JUST LIKE THE LAST TIME!**

BUT **THIS** TIME, SHE **RECOGNIZES** SOME-THING IN THOSE BALE-FUL EYES. THIS TIME, SHE **KNOWS...**

...**KNOWS** THAT TED SALLIS MUST HAVE IN-JECTED **HIMSELF** WITH HIS SUPER-SOLDIER SERUM TO PREVENT A.I.M. FROM STEALING IT...

...**KNOWS** THAT IT MUST HAVE COMBINED WITH WEIRD CHEMICALS IN THE SWAMP TO TURN HIM INTO THIS **MAN-THING.**

Man Thing's origin is revisited by Tony Isabella and Vicente Alcazar in "All the Faces of Fear!" from Monsters Unleashed! V1#5 (April 1974) Marvel Comics Group

tles as *Journey into Unknown Worlds* [1950–57], *Marvel Tales* [1949–57], *Menace* [1953–54], and *Uncanny Tales* [1952–57], and—due to their pre-Code nature—could not be published in the standard four-color comic format without risking the CCA's wrath. As time went on, the reprints were eventually dropped.) Bridging the pieces would be full page monster movie stills bearing introductory captions, which were useless except as marred photos. (EC, with the Crypt-Keeper and her siblings, and later Warren with Cousin Eerie and Uncle Creepy, were much more successful in such attempts, as their host-like mascots were far more personable and usually integrated into the story itself, if only as a wraparound.)

The first of these horror comic magazines to see the light of dusk was *Dracula Lives!* (1973–75). Boasting an early painted cover by Boris Vallejo, this title included several stories featuring the antihero from Marvel's color comic series *The Tomb of Dracula* (which was begat a year earlier and ran until 1979). Most of the reprints

in *Dracula Lives!* dealt with the undead, and the articles were all devoted to Dracula's kith and kin, both onscreen and off.

Although Marvel's interpretation was far more characteristic than previous takes on Bram Stoker's creation, the stories in Marvel's magazine suffered from serious inconsistencies, due to the art and writing chores constantly changing hands. (Whatever faults it may have had, the highly regarded seventy issue comic book run of *Tomb of Dracula* did not suffer such a fate, as it was illustrated from start to finish by Eugene Colan, with writer Marvin Wolfman on board for almost as long.) Furthermore, the vampire lord as perceived in the magazine was not as emphatic as he should have been, since he carried much of the book by himself. Whereas, say, Christopher Lee's Dracula had an aristocratic air about him, Marvel's Count—with his lofty deliveries and pretentious assumptions—often came off as pompous. Whilst Bela Lugosi's Dracula had a certain class, Marvel's Count was simply crass.

Marv Wolfman and Neal Adams "reinvent" Stoker's bloodsucker in "That Dracula May Live Again."
Dracula Lives! V1#2 (1973) Marvel Comics Group

There were exceptions, as in the case of Count Dracula's origin story that appeared in *Dracula Lives!'* second issue. Written by Marv Wolfman and illustrated by Neal Adams, 'That Dracula May Live Again!' captured Stoker's vision in a way that pedestrian efforts couldn't, bestowing a certain dignity upon the character that was often sorely lacking. Starting in the fifth issue, the editors decided to actually take a crack at the source material of the magazine's namesake, introducing a serialized adaptation of Stoker's novel. Adequately produced by Roy Thomas and Dick Giordano, it was a nice primer for younger fans unfamiliar with the book; for those of us who already had intimate knowledge of Stoker's literary classic, it proved to be little more than filler.

Towards the end of *Dracula Lives!* another feature character was introduced, Dracula's own daughter Lilith. Unlike her old world father, Lilith was presented in a more mod fashion, and even sported a costume not unlike a typical Marvel superheroine. A far more sympathetic monster than her father, Lilith took no pleasure in drinking the blood of innocents, preferring to prowl the seedier districts of the city and milk the life from such undesirables as rapists and drug dealers. When not laying waste to the metaphorical scum of the earth, her spirit resided in the body of the unwary Irish immigrant Angel O'Hara. Although readers could more readily identify with her on several levels, the character rarely amounted to more than a second rate Vampirella. Still, many of the stories were engaging, and benefited from the continuity.

Within a few months of the premiere of *Dracula Lives!* Marvel had a modest stable of b&w horror magazines that also included *Monsters Unleashed!*, *Tales of the Zombie* and *Vampire Tales*, each catering to a different breed of beast (although *Monsters Unleashed!* was much less discriminating than its elitist siblings).

Monsters Unleashed! (1973–75) gave coverage to several already established characters, from Marvel's takes on classic movie monsters (Frankenstein's Monster and Werewolf by Night among them) to more 'original' creations (the Man-Thing reprint 'At the Stroke of Midnight' (v1#2), which displayed Jim Steranko's mastery of sequential art; to the original (albeit anti-climactic) 'The Vampire Wants Blood' (v1#5), by regulars Moench and Mayerick, Marvel made some valiant attempts to match the level of quality that was Warren's watershed, and occasionally succeeded.

The following year, Marvel Comics decided to expand its line of b&w magazines. The first, *The Haunt of Horror* (1974–75), started as yet another supernatural horror anthology, but by the second issue the editors sharpened its focus. Driven by the ongoing serializations of Gabriel the Devil Hunter, Marvel sought to cash in on the growing interest in demonic possession fueled by William Friedkin's blockbuster *The Exorcist* (1974) and the William Blatty book that inspired it. At the same time Gabriel made his debut, Satana had found a much more accommodating home within the pages of *The Haunt of Horror* as well.

Gabriel (his surname was never revealed to the reader) is an ex-priest who gives up preaching for full time soul saving having successfully cast an evil spirit from himself, at the cost of his faith and his right eye. Aided by his female assistant Desadia, who boasts some premonitory powers, Gabriel spends each issue going through the motions, having turned exorcism into a rather dull, predictable science. It's difficult to lay the blame at the writer's feet, considering the inherent limitations of the demonic possession subgenre. (Writer Moench makes the claim in an editorial that, while writing the Gabriel stories, he was plagued by a series of obviously supernatural occurrences, much like Blatty said he was when writing his novel, and the cast and crew of Friedkin's film. These tongue in cheek assertions are a much better read than many of the stories themselves.)

With an eye towards evil spirits and the devil himself, the rest of the stories were equally turgid or trite, and would only perturb those readers who

Hmmm… Jad's cover art looks kind of familiar, don't you think? The Haunt of Horror V1#3 (September 1974) Marvel Comics Group

took Ouija boards seriously. The only truly shocking thing that could be found within its pages was the occasional stab at a taboo subject (e.g. incest), but the handling seemed just as gratuitous as the watered down epithets. Artistically, most of the stories were sub par, although the series did boast a few nice covers, in particular Jad's contribution to the third issue. Harkening back in some respect to the weird menace pulps, the deliciously painted cover depicted several rotting corpses lumbering out of a swamp to accost a hapless victim cowering in a provocatively torn dress.

The second new horror magazine to be published by Marvel that year, *Monsters of the Movies* (1974–75), was not an oversized comic, but was instead cast in the mold of *Famous Monsters of Filmland* (1958–83). Forgoing illustrated stories for articles on and reviews of horror films, *Monsters of the Movies* gave its inspiration a run for

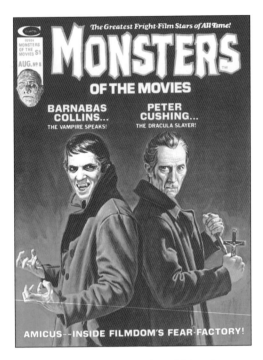

A showdown between Jonathan Frid's Barnabas
Collins and Peter Cushing's van Helsing?
Only in the dreams of a desperate seven-year old.
Cover art by Bob Larkin for Monsters of the Movies
V1#8 (August 1975) Marvel Comics Group

its money with well written pieces, collections
of rare stills, and up to the minute film coverage.
Ultimately, though, it simply could not compete
with a magazine that had established itself seven-
teen years earlier; Monsters of the Movie's fate was
the same as the many other fan magazines that
fought for shelf space on magazine racks during
the horror glut of the mid seventies.

The staff of Monsters of the Movies remained
stable throughout its run, and included two writers who had made something of a name for themselves outside Marvel and the magazine industry.
The first, Donald F Glut (1944–), was the crea-
tor of the exceptional Gold Key horror comic The
Occult Files of Doctor Spektor (1973–77). Today,
Glut writes and directs his own independent
horror and exploitation films with titles like The

Erotic Rites of Countess Dracula (2001) and The
Mummy's Kiss (2003). The second, Ron Hay-
dock (1940–77), was also an actor who appeared
in several of Ray Dennis Steckler's no budget
efforts, including Rat Pfink a Boo Boo (1965),
Lemon Grove Kids Meet the Monster (1965), Body
Fever (1969) and Blood Shack (1971). Sadly, Ron
died in a hit and run accident only a few years
after his respectable stint on the magazine.

There were several other Marvel titles that
only made it an issue or two before being cancelled in 1975. Masters of Terror featured illustrated versions of horror classics by the likes of
Robert Bloch, Robert E Howard and HP Lovecraft. Most readers were probably put off by the
fact that most of these stories were reprints less
than a year or two old (much like the annuals
produced for many of the Marvel horror magazines). Legion of Monsters made an effort to pick
up where Dracula Lives! and Monsters Unleashed!
left off, continuing the Frankenstein and Dracula
cycles that were started therein, but it didn't survive past the first issue.

That same year, Marvel Comics started the
self referential Marvel Preview, a publication that
devoted each issue to a different character or subject. Four of these issues would hold interest to
fans of Marvel's horror outings. The first (v1#3)
was devoted to Blade, the Vampire Slayer; the second (v1#8)—a continuation of the cancelled Legion of Monsters—also included Blade as well as
Morbius; the third (v1#12) was a continuation of
The Haunt of Horror and featured Lilith, Daughter of Dracula; and the last (v1#16) was titularly
the third issue of Masters of Terror, although it
included a story with Lilith and strayed from the
classics presented in its predecessors.

The eighth issue of Marvel Preview included
an overview of the short-lived run of Marvel's
b&w horror publications, written by a chap who
had written voluminous letters that appeared in

Advertisement for and cover art by Frank Kelly Freas for the aborted The Haunt of Horror V1#3 (1973) Marvel Comics Group

himself with more lighthearted fantasy and sci fi illustrations.

Not surprisingly, some of the stories slated for the ultimately canned issue later appeared as prose only pieces in the illustrated second series of *The Haunt of Horror*. In the editorial for the first magazine sized issue, the reader is told flat out that its previous prose heavy incarnation simply flopped. Although the field of sci fi had been supporting innumerable digest sized fiction magazines since the demise of the pulps in the fifties, horror fans of the seventies were apparently more visual, as every attempt to do the same for this genre would—by this time—fold after only a few issues. Thus, despite Marvel's best attempt to produce a quality product, it was a sad fact that the market simply couldn't bear it…at least to their satisfaction.

For quite a few years now, high grade copies of these two publications have fetched a tidy sum on the collector's market due to their scarcity and the names involved, many of whom had yet to establish themselves as fan favorites. Since many of the best stories were reprints or later collected in paperback anthologies, one could probably assume that the casual readers of fantastic fiction tended not to hold onto their copies. Additionally, the most fervent of collectors from the time—comic book fans—had little use for the prose format. In essence, these odd ducks were discarded and forgotten, an uncharacteristic attempt by Marvel to break out of the comic related fields with which their name had become synonymous.

❏ Marvel monster magazine checklist, see page 285
❏ Marvel monster magazine artist & writer checklist, see page 286
❏ *The Haunt of Horror* digest index, see page 284

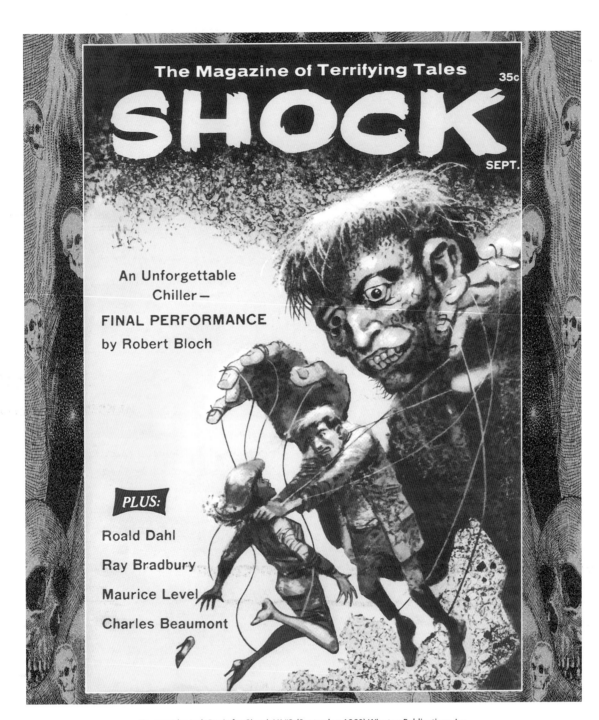

Cover art by Jack Davis for Shock V1#3 (September 1960) Winston Publications, Inc.

CUT DOWN TO SIZE

THE GOLDEN AGE OF HORROR DIGEST MAGAZINES

In a sense, it is unfortunate that the story I must now relate should be so largely a thing of undetermined shadows, of half shaped hints and forbidden inferences. Otherwise, it could never be written by human hand or read by human eye. My own slight part in this hideous drama was limited to its last act; and to me its earlier scenes were merely a remote and ghastly legend.

Excerpt from 'The Nameless Offspring' by Clark Ashton Smith, *Magazine of Horror* v6#3 (Summer 1970) Acme Publishing/ Health Knowledge, Inc.

THE SIXTIES saw a resurgence of interest in the horror genre, although American publications devoted to weird fiction still struggled, overwhelmed by the sci fi and detective magazines that dominated the market. Titles like *Fantastic* (1952–80), *Galaxy Sci fi* (1950–95) and *Worlds of If* (1952–72) shared newsstand space with *Alfred Hitchcock's Mystery Magazine* (1956–) and *Ellery Queen's Mystery Magazine* (1941–), but this left little room on the shelf for the less appreciated genres, all of which were descendents of the pulp magazines that had flourished only a few decades before.

The earlier part of the twentieth century saw the growth of the pulp magazine, a label that has since been applied to a style of writing made popular by the format. The originator of the pulp format, Frank Munsey (1854–1925), is quoted as saying, "the story is worth more than the paper it is printed on." These periodicals—roughly 7" x 10" and printed on economical and thus highly acidic paper stock—were the literary equivalent of comic books and moving pictures: a cheap, mass market form of disposable entertainment geared towards the lower and middle class. By the thirties, pulps had acquired a mass appeal, touching upon a wide range of demographics. Some genres were gender specific, romance and men's adventure being two polar examples, and although most pulps were intended for adults, it wasn't uncommon for a title to hold some appeal to younger readers. In the years to come, these magazines would garner a bad reputation due to a handful of titles aimed specifically at a misogynistic male market, undoubtedly a backlash in response to the growing woman's movement. Pulps devoted to horror and weird fiction were no exception, and were (directly or indirectly) responsible for what would now be rightfully considered politically incorrect entertainment.

With America's involvement in WWII, paper shortages forced publishers to trim down the size of their periodicals; by the fifties, all but a few were published in a more condensed digest format, still utilized by publishers to this day. The fifties also saw a newfound conservatism, which quashed those titles geared towards the public's more prurient interests.

During the reign of the pulps, horror was generally referred to as weird fiction, and encompassed everything from traditional supernatural

Pulp predecessor to the horror digests.. Strange Stories V4#2
(October 1940) Better Publications Inc

two key selling points. In this case, the beloved foundations of American entertainment were defined by nubile and obviously vulnerable young women in various stages of undress—whatever clothes remaining often tattered and just barely concealing their perky (i.e. gravity defying) headlights—being accosted by deformed (i.e. impotent) masterminds or steroid-ridden evildoers in masks who could never get a date in high school because they were just too dang creepy. Torture devices—traditional Spanish or even state of the art—littered the scene, usually a basement or cave or similarly dank environment where the inhuman killers could carry out their perverse pleasures without interference. The muscled superhero could often be seen in the background, desperate to reach his shackled prize but distracted by half human beasts or maladjusted cultists. One needn't be Freud to see exactly what drove some sexually immature readers into the arms of the weird menace pulps.

Despite the abundance of these sordid outings, more traditionally macabre fiction still had a place among the pulp readership. Much of it continued the American tradition that Edgar Allan Poe (1809–49) had initiated the previous century, although those stories that evoked anything in the way of real poetry were, not surprisingly, sparse. At its best, pulp horror fiction was literate, imaginative and engaging. At its worst, it was not far removed from the gothic chapbooks and penny dreadfuls of the nineteenth century.

Most of the titles devoted to weird fiction had modest runs; *Strange Tales of Mystery & Terror* (1931–33), *Horror Stories* (1935–41), *Strange Stories* (1939–41), *Unknown* (1939–43), and *Famous Fantastic Mysteries* (1939–53) are a few examples of those whose impact was more than negligible. The most esteemed and influential, *Weird Tales* (1923–54), boasts a longevity denied its peers, thanks to its persistent and unrivaled

fiction to the sexually aggressive 'weird menace' fare. The latter was a sub-genre very specific to the thirties, which invariably had women abducted and tortured by inhuman villains armed with insidious devices or supernatural powers, while the story's low rent hero made his way to the killer's lair delayed by various traps, or forced into mortal combat with monstrous creatures or more mundane minions. These weird menace pulps were extremely popular in their time, but this had little to do with the surefire combination of cross genre elements; what defined them were the lurid covers, which often depicted a scene in the story to which all the action was leading the reader, if indeed it was employed at all.

Suffice to say, these covers would immediately catch the ready eye of many male readers browsing the newsstand, as sex and violence were their level of quality (it was revived no less than twice, once in the seventies, then again in the eighties).

This series was almost singlehandedly responsible for kickstarting the careers of such notable fantasy writers as Seabury Quinn (1889–1964), Clark Ashton Smith (1893–1961), Robert E Howard (1906–36), August Derleth (1909–71), Robert Bloch (1917–94), Henry S Whitehead, and—of course—a man whose name is inadvertently synonymous with the publication, Howard Phillips Lovecraft (1890–1937). *Weird Tales* also benefited from artistry by the likes of J Allen St John (1872–1957), Hannes Bok (1914–64), Virgil Finlay (1914–71), Frank Kelly Freas, and the inexhaustible Margaret Brundage (1900–76), whose exquisitely painted covers are as inseparable from the publication as is Lovecraft's prose.

Unfortunately, the fifties were not a prosperous time for traditional horror. In film, the genre had been all but absorbed by sci fi, re-inventing itself in the guise of alien beings intent on wiping out mankind and having their way with our women, or giant insects mutated by atomic radiation that viewed our species as an all-you-can-eat buffet. In comics, the Kefauver Senate Hearings and Comics Code Authority had emasculated the genre, leaving it an impotent, practically unmarketable commodity free of the depiction of walking corpses that was somehow responsible for the growing scourge of juvenile delinquency. In fiction, it fared little better. With the demise of *Weird Tales* in 1954, weird fiction suffered its greatest blow, leaving only the occasional paperback anthology to fill the void.

In 1960, two attempts were made to revitalize the tradition of weird fiction and capitalize on the growing interest in all things horror. Unfortunately, these two periodicals, *Fear!* ("Tales of the Terror-Filled Unknown") and *Shock* ("The Magazine of Terrifying Tales"), have between them only five issues that never breached another

Cover art by "GAP" for Fear! V1#1 (May 1960)
Great American Publications, Inc.

year. Both titles were introduced in May of 1960, *Fear!* boasting a grisly painted cover depicting a scarecrow making short work of its eponymous prey, and *Shock* featuring a striking three-color, pen and ink illustration by ex-EC Comics artist Jack Davis. Both of these pint sized magazines featured an array of both burgeoning and established writers, newer unpublished fiction alongside classic reprints that even dated back to the previous century.

It is no surprise, though, that *Shock* outlived *Fear!*, even if it was only by one issue. Whereas the first issue of *Fear!* filled its pages with work by Wilkie Collins (1824–89), John Jakes (1932–) and Hal Ellison, whilst *Shock* had the likes of Anthony Boucher né William Anthony Parker White (1911–68), Ray Bradbury (1920–) and Theodore Sturgeon gracing theirs. (Much of the

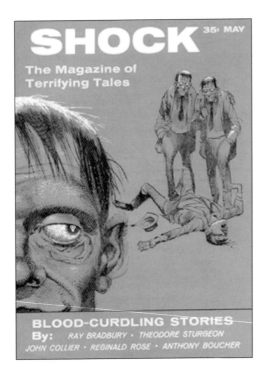

Cover art by Jack Davis for Shock V1#1
(May 1960) Winston Publications, Inc.

material in *Shock* was reprinted from the afore-mentioned pulp magazines, but had been long out of print by the time it resurfaced here.) The artwork in both titles was sparse and unexceptional, but *Shock* had the upper hand with the occasional Davis spot illustration.

The second outing for *Fear!* proved its last gasp; this was not surprising, in that it boasted almost nothing in the way of saleable names. *Shock*'s second issue, on the other hand, offered more (and more inspired) work by Davis in addition to a similarly impressive list of wordsmiths. The third issue of *Shock* continued the tradition of excellence, but alas, it was insufficient to establish a readership that would carry it into a new year.

In 1963 and 1966, two very notable weird fiction titles were published by one Health Knowledge, Inc aka Acme. Although the publisher's bread and butter was the girlie magazines

churned out under their more 'hygienic' imprint throughout the sixties, they were also responsible for a number of digest magazines which included sci fi (*Famous Sci fi*), crime fiction (*Chase*), men's adventure (*World Wide Adventure*), and parapsychology (*Exploring the Unknown*). (They were also behind the short-lived monster magazine *Shriek*—covered in more detail in the next section of this book—and sex manuals like *The Real Life Guide to Sex & Marriage*, which was probably how they established themselves, if the "Health Knowledge, Inc." is any indication.) All their fiction titles were published in an atypical format, slightly smaller than the average digest publication and stapled instead of squarebound.

The first publication from Acme, *Magazine of Horror* (1963–71), carried the terse cover subtitle of "Bizarre ◆ Frightening ◆ Gruesome" and the contents page expanded upon it by claiming its penchant for "The Bizarre and the Unusual" but to be more specific, the focus was on gothic and outright supernatural fare. The *Magazine of Horror* started out offering a good balance of new material and vintage reprints, but it was later weighted down with stories in its thirty six issue run that were originally printed in such pulp magazines as *Weird Tales* and *Strange Tales*. (With very little diligence, the reader could find the small print disclaimer in the indicia: "While the greatest diligence has been used to ascertain the owners of rights, and to secure necessary permissions, the editor and publisher wish to offer their apologies in any possible case of accidental infringements." Although copyright infringement wasn't the issue then as it has been in recent years, the publishers were obviously trying to cover their ass if it turned out one of the 'borrowed' pieces wasn't actually in the public domain.)

Like many other Acme digest sized periodicals at the time, the earlier issues of *Magazine of Horror* bore text only covers, which undoubtedly hurt

ral contrivances. Not surprisingly, there was a crossover of many of the same writers between the two books, which may be why many people assume them to be companion magazines even though both were from different publishers.

Aside from the occasional unpublished Robert E Howard story, *Coven 13* [Camelot Publishing] (1969–70)—which had a bent for dark fantasy—eschewed the oft recycled pulp stories for new fiction from the likes of Harlan Ellison and Ron Goulart. Both the painted covers and the interior illustrations were supplied entirely by newcomer William Stout (1949–), who would later make a name for himself with numerous beautifully illustrated books devoted to his first love, dinosaurs, as well as his work as a production designer in Hollywood.

In 1971, with only four issues to its name, *Coven 13*'s subscription list was bought out by Fantasy Publishing Company, the editorship changed, and the title slagged for the more generic *Witchcraft & Sorcery*. With the fifth issue, it also dispensed with the digest format for that of a standard magazine, although it was often printed with a newsprint cover stock for economical reasons. Despite some great contributions—including early work from artists Berni Wrightson and Jeff Jones—it folded after six more issues.

In the early seventies, some attempted to continue the tradition with material of a higher literary content. *The Haunt of Horror* [Marvel Comics Group] (1973)—covered elsewhere in this book—and the resurrected *Weird Tales* [Renown Publications] (1973–74) were two, but neither one had the opportunity to establish or re-establish itself. *Weird Tales*' second attempt at life was a brief respite from the grave, lasting only four issues. (Coincidentally, the last four issues of the original run published from 1953 to 1954 were also in the digest format. When it was resuscitated in 1981 by Kensington Publishing, it

Whips and chains, anyone?
Uncredited cover art for Web Terror Stories V5#2
(June 1965) Candar Publishing Company, Inc.

was redefined as a slick take on the original, larger pulps, undoubtedly to avoid the curse that befell the first two series. Third time's a charm, as *Weird Tales* is still being published to this day, although it has undergone numerous editor and publisher changes along the way.) *Weird Tales* the second offered a nice balance of new stories and previously published efforts, and introduced to new readers such luminary contributors as Lovecraft, Howard, Bradbury, Finlay, William Hope Hodgson (1877–1918), Abraham Merritt (1884–1943), Clark Ashton Smith (1893–1961) and Frank Belknap Long (1903–94) as well as relative newcomers

Taking its cues from Acme's 'thrifty' approach to publishing, *Weird Mystery* [Ultimate Publishing Company] (1970–71) was another short-lived title that dished up pulp reprints, all excavated from Ziff-Davis Publishing Company's vast archives, mostly culled from *Fantastic* (1952–80) and *Fantastic Adventures* (1939–53). Although it probably didn't have much appeal to those horror fans thirsting for outings with a more modern flavor—lasting only four issues may be an indication of how dated the material had become by the seventies—these stories were accompanied by the original illustrations that graced them upon their initial publication. Unfortunately, the illustrations did little to make *Weird Mystery* a pleasant visual experience, as the text was tiny, and the contents were crammed in such a way that everything threatened to be pushed off the edge of the page when it didn't actually bleed over.

As the seventies progressed, the growing markets of paperback anthologies and small press magazines filled much of the demand for short horror fiction. A handful of aspiring publishers would continue to try their hand at the format for years to come; although a few have made valiant attempts to produce a digest periodical, newsstand distribution has proved nigh impossible for such small print publications. Having crossed into the world of online publishing, webzines have become the favored means to print and peruse through short horror fiction, accessible to anyone with an internet connection and a few hours to spare. As it pertains to weird fiction, mass market digests have now been relegated to a nostalgic realm shared and lorded over by its precursor, the pulp magazine, but they have yet to gain the recognition that is otherwise afforded their oversized ancestors.

❏ **Horror digest magazine checklist, see page 296**

directly or indirectly influenced by the style of fiction to which *Weird Tales* was seminal.

Weird Tales' brief run in the seventies—which lasted all of four issues—was edited by the late Sam Moskowitz (1920–97), who during his lifetime was considered the foremost expert in the field of sci fi. Around the time he oversaw Renown's short-lived periodical, Moskowitz also edited numerous, very successful, anthologies devoted to short form horror fiction—*Ghostly by Gaslight* (1971) [Pyramid Books] and *Horrors Unknown* (1971) [Berkley Medallion Books] among them—several of which were co-edited with Alden H Norton. Unfortunately, due to the magazine's poor distribution, Moskowitz was forced to abandon what was undoubtedly a dream come true for him both as an editor and fan.

❏ **Horror digest magazine checklist, see page 296**

Cover art for Shriek! V1#1 (May 1965) Acme News Company, Inc.

Here is the first issue of a great new Monster Horror Magazine SHRIEK. Within these pages, you will find terror—the menace of witch, warlock, and flesh eater, the lurking fear of the undead, the horror of man's inhumanity to man.

Excerpt from the editorial of *Shriek!* v1#1 (May 1965) Acme Publishing Company/ Health Knowledge, Inc.

MOST OF US grew up reading Warren's *Famous Monsters of Filmland*, and although each issue rarely sated our thirst for all things horror, our limited allowances dictated our inability to buy each and every magazine on the newsstand that touted itself as 'the' monster magazine. Despite the allure of the other garish covers staring back at us, *Famous Monsters* always came first. If there was money left over not spent on comic books, then maybe…

Once the market proved receptive to publisher Jim Warren and editor Forrest J Ackerman's groundbreaking monster magazine, it was inevitable that other struggling publishers would try their hand at the formula. Investigative articles weren't necessary to sell a periodical aimed at young horror fans. Simply fill most of the pages with reproductions of film stills obtained free of charge from studios desperate to promote their low budget creature features, accompanied by some vaguely witty captions pasted on by a bored typesetter, and voila! A hit with the kids. The ones that liked monsters, anyway.

The sixties were rife with pale *Famous Monsters* imitations, but none exhibited the knowledge and sincerity that Forry and his fellow writers displayed. Those that did, produced by serious aficionados, were often too heady for the younger readers, the cornerstone of monster magazine sales. Also, many publications simply did not have the distribution of Warren's flagship book. Monster magazines were springing out of the woodwork, but would just as quickly disappear.

The innocuously named Acme News Company, Inc. aka Health Knowledge, Inc. had already established itself with weird fiction digests like *Magazine of Horror* and *Startling Mystery Stories*, both of which depended on reprints from pulp magazines, as discussed in the previous chapter. The publisher's primary source of income, however, was from a variety of short-lived girlie magazines they churned out during the sixties (*Mod Chicks, Nifties*), several of which were devoted to sexploitation films (*Raw Flix, Untamed Cinema*).

It was not unheard of for struggling or spurious magazine publishers to run the gamut from all ages fare to skin magazines. (Stanley Publishing, known for such low rent comic horrors as *Chilling Tales of Horror, Ghoul Tales, Shock* and *Stark Terror* had also explored the world of stapled navels with titles like *Rugged* and *Satan* in the late fifties. Even Jim Warren attempted to ride *Playboy*'s coattails in 1957 with his own girlie magazine, *After Hours*, which only lasted five issues but got him hauled into court on obscenity charges.)

Uncredited cover art for Shriek! V1#2
(October 1965) Acme News Company, Inc.

Uncredited cover art for Shriek! V1#3
(Summer 1966) Acme News Company, Inc.

The premiere issue of *Shriek!* heralded its arrival with a preface that attempted to set the tone for issues to come. Although the focus was on supernatural cinema, the contents occasionally strayed from the magazine's own mission statement. As for exploiting man's inhumanity to man, *Shriek!* made a valiant attempt to go where its peers dared not to at the time, as we'll see shortly.

It is not surprising that the majority of the films covered in *Shriek!* were produced in the UK; even though it was primarily distributed in the United States by Acme, *Shriek!* was actually designed by the House of Horror in London. (Even if one hadn't read the small type in the indicia, the abundance of Anglo fare, and the fact that many of the reviews included both UK and US release titles was something of a dead giveaway.)

The film reviews were little more than blow by blow accounts of the events, *including* the shock endings. Spoilers aside, those looking for a subjective critique or behind the scenes accounts would find nothing to hold their interest. (No bylines are given for these glorified synopses, which gives one the impression that many of the pieces were probably ghosted by the editor himself.)

Shriek! did provide some engaging interviews with the likes of Boris Karloff, Christopher Lee and Vincent Price, but these dialogues had been abandoned by the time the fourth and last issue saw print. The only real articles included an unfinished history of the horror film (although it appeared in the first issue, part two never saw print) and an aimless piece with a similar bent (which closes the last issue, and which actually appears to have been sent to press incomplete).

207

Advertisement for Shriek Monster Masks, a steal at two dollars each, from Globe Sales.

In the first issue, *Shriek!* ran coverage on a film to be released in the United States as *The House at the End of the World*, although it would bear the title of *The Tomb of Ligeia* for the UK market. In the following issue, the editor claimed that they had been misinformed, and that this longwinded title had instead been 'saved' for a new Boris Karloff movie which was then reviewed in their usual unaffected fashion. This movie, though, was ultimately released as *Die, Monster, Die!* in the States, making one seriously question their credibility. (If Karloff himself hadn't referred to the production as *The House at the End of the World* in his interview, one would have written them off as entirely incompetent.)

The magazine did have one thing that set it apart from its competitors. Unlike *Famous Monsters* and the slew of imitations, *Shriek!* would devote several pages of each issue to non genre films that flaunted censors and openly displayed barbaric cruelty or sadism. Presumably, the publishers noticed the growing interest in films of an explicitly violent nature (HG Lewis' cinematic atrocities had already been making waves) and sought to capitalize on the trend.

The first issue spotlighted some particularly grisly stills from the POW film *The Secret of Blood Island* (1965) and the Japanese import *Seppuku* (1962) aka *Harakiri*, or belly-slitting, which lived up to the film's title with its gruesome finale. The second issue ran a selection of gruesome scenes from such non horror films as *Lord Jim*, *She* and *The War Lord* (all 1965). Most of these stills depicted people bound and tortured, and were justified with an introduction that asked, "Is violence really necessary?" The editor then insisted that, after seeing the photos, the readers should judge for themselves if such scenes were gratuitous. Under the subtle headline of "Blood Galore," issue three spotlighted some increasingly bloody scenes from *Genghis Khan* (1965).

The last issue shied away from any non horror carnage, but snuck in some brief nudity that undoubtedly concerned a few parents.

In retrospect, one can't help but find the editorial in the fourth and last issue amusing. Penned by one 'Frank N Stein,' our host—silent in previous issues—considers the bleak outlook of horror films in 1966. (One wonders if he foresaw the magazine's imminent demise, and sought a scapegoat.) He then blames this decline of monster movies on the rising popularity of spy films and *The Sound of Music*, the defanging of the genre with spoofs like *The Munsters*, and Hammer's abandonment of the genre for epics like *She*.

Considering that the fifties were a low point for supernatural horror fare, that television shows like *The Addams Family* helped create a resurgence of interest in monster mania, and that Hammer's output was primarily horror until the company finally dissolved at the close of the seventies, one questions the editor's grasp of the genre his magazine purported to support. Considering *Shriek!*'s loose definition of horror, in the years it was published there was obviously no shortage of material for them to exploit.

Despite its faults, *Shriek!* is fondly remembered by some fans who grew up in the sixties. (Up until a few years ago when a large batch of uncirculated copies was unearthed, all four issues demanded a premium on the collector's market, in any condition. Today, high grade copies can be had for about twenty dollars apiece.) The exclusive interviews, the assortment of still photos, and even the ads featuring monster toys not available from Warren's mail order outfit Captain Company, make them worth owning. And, despite the devotion to "the horror of man's inhumanity to man," *Shriek!* retains a sense of naivety that could have only been fostered in the sixties.

❏ *Shriek!* magazine index, see page 297

Uncredited cover art for House of Horror #1 (April 1978) Warren Publishing Company

WARREN'S HASTILY ERECTED HOUSE OF HORROR

I N THE EARLY months of 1978, in the back pages of their various publications, the juggernaut known as Warren Publishing Company announced with very little fanfare the premiere issue of *House of Horror*, purportedly a new quarterly publication that—like its flagship book *Famous Monsters of Filmland*—focused on fantastic cinema. This first issue was made available only through Warren's in-house mail order business, Captain Company; such a promotion was not unlike them, as they had released several other magazines that eschewed newsstands entirely, namely *The Spirit Color Special* in 1975 and *Vampirella Color Special* in 1977. (Due to the limited print runs and availability, these remain some of the most sought after books published by Warren in the seventies.) Some avid readers at the time probably assumed the limited distribution was responsible for *House of Horror* never making it to a second issue, but they would have been wrong: Jim Warren never intended a follow up.

There was never a shortage of publishers trying to compete with *Famous Monsters*, but aside from a few exceptions most of their books died within a few years. Comic book publisher Charlton Publications tried their hand with *Horror Monsters* and *Mad Monsters*, but these interchangeable titles amounted to ten issues published between 1961 and 1965. *The Monster Times* [The Monster Times Publishing Company] (1972–76), an oversized foldout tabloid that was just as quick to cover modern shockers like *Shriek of the Mu-*

tilated as it was Hollywood's golden age horrors, offered a cheap and enjoyable alternative to the more traditional monster magazines of the time. Far more extraordinary is *Castle of Frankenstein* [Gothic Castle Publishing Company] (1962–75), a headier publication with twenty six issues to its credit, which, much like *Famous Monsters*, was revived in recent years.

One of *Famous Monsters'* more fondly remembered peers was not an American publication, but the UK periodical *House of Hammer* [Top Sellers, Ltd], which ran from 1976 through 1984, albeit under a number of variant titles. Wanting to break into the American market, they announced plans to expand their distribution to include the US and change the name of the magazine to the less exclusive *(Hammer's) House of Horror*. With Hammer Studios having lost its foothold with American filmgoers, they felt many of the younger American readers wouldn't pick up on the reference to the senescent production company.

Competition from other American publications was undoubtedly expected, but it is doubtful that Top Sellers had any clue just how bloody a battle it would prove to be, and that their attempts to expand would be singlehandedly cut down by the publisher of rival magazine *Famous Monsters of Filmland*, James 'Jim' Warren.

Inarguably, Warren was responsible for some of the most highly regarded and influential horror magazines of the sixties and seventies, both film and comic, and it is impossible to offer a retrospective on either without paying homage. His vision and dedication to showcase the best work on the market clearly demonstrated his passion for the field; this passion, however, was also responsible for his precarious personal and working relationships. Many creators have noted his volatile nature, particularly when it came to the competition, but even those freelance writers and artists working for him were often subjected

Cover art by Brian Lewis for House of Horror V1#1
(March 1978) Top Sellers, Ltd.

Cover art by Ramon Sola for House of Horror
V2#7/#19 (April 1978) Top Sellers, Ltd.

to his umbrage, especially if their loyalty to the company was at all in question. Although his cut-throat approach to business was at least partially responsible for the quality of his magazines, it made him few friends.

With the word out that Top Sellers were intending to edge their way into the American marketplace, the publisher of *Famous Monsters* decided to take immediate action. Jim Warren didn't fancy the idea of the competition in the least, and so he decided to make things difficult for the less established publishing house. Before the first issue of Top Sellers' publication reached these shores, Warren had rushed to press a one-off with the same title, thus securing a copyright on it before the London based publisher could make the claim. Warren immediately filed for copyright infringement, and the case was taken to court. While the trial was underway, Top Sellers released the first issue of their magazine aimed at

the American market; unbeknownst to readers, it was composed entirely of reprints (including the cover art, which was borrowed from the seventeenth issue of *House of Hammer*).

Still duking it out in court, the next issue of the regular series, number nineteen, bore the new much coveted title as well, and even received some limited distribution within the US. Unfortunately, the courts upheld Warren's claim, so Top Sellers was forced to change the title again, this time to *(Hammer's) Halls of Horror* with issue twenty. Despite the fact that the UK magazine was in many ways superior to Warren's monster movie magazines—particularly in the writing and the depth of its film coverage—there never was a second issue of the US only version, and issue twenty proved to be the last with any overseas distribution at all. Three issues later, the title was cancelled, although it was revived in 1982 by another publisher, Quality Communications, which put out another eight issues before that series issued its last gasp.

Much like the fabled *Eerie* #1 (Sep 1965), Warren only printed enough copies of *House of Horror* in order to secure the claim—200 to 400 copies, by most accounts. This sober estimate makes it the second rarest Warren publication, beaten only by *Eerie*, for which there were less than 200 copies made. Whereas the first issue of *Eerie* was hastily Xeroxed and only sold through a newsstand inhabiting the same building as the offices of Warren Publishing Company, this *House of Horror* one-shot boasted top notch production values and was far more accessible to the public.

Those readers who plunked down money for this magazine that could be had for a dollar post paid were no doubt disappointed by what awaited them in the mailbox a month later. Although the quality of the cover and paper stock was better than anything Warren had ever used to print their flagship book, this new title was nothing more than a hurried paste-up of reprints from *Famous Monsters*. Furthermore, the magazine ran only thirty two pages—the same as most comic books at the time—which was a far cry from *Famous Monsters*, whose girth was at least double that. Most disheartening, the 'horror' in the title was a misnomer, as the book spent more time dwelling on sci fi fare than monster movies, in particular *Star Wars* and *Close Encounters of the Third Kind*.

Even if Warren's *House of Horror* had sold well, it is doubtful he would have kept it going. Establishing a second horror film magazine would have only drawn sales away from *Famous Monsters*, which by this time had to offer more focus on films like *Star Wars* to compete in a marketplace that was losing interest in all things horror.

Today, copies of this magazine typically fetch a couple hundred dollars in high grade condition; although rare, it isn't too difficult to track down a copy. Of course, this is easy for me to say as I

Cover art by Bill Phillips for House of Horror
V2#8/#20 (May 1978) Top Sellers, Ltd.

have seen more copies of this book in one place than most people ever will. In the late eighties, I worked for a local bookstore owner who acquired a large collection of horror magazines through an auction that included no less than fifty copies of this magazine; how the previous owner—having died in a house fire, hence the liquidation of his entire collection—had gotten his hands on so many copies is anybody's guess. Unfortunately, my employer and I sold off most of the copies before the marketplace got wind of their scarcity, so a large chunk of the print run—a fourth to an eighth of it, at the very least—was primarily circulated in western Washington. Alas, neither of us has any copies left.

❑ *House of Horror* content & credits, see page 298

Top Excerpt from L'Amante del Vampiro (1960) Ken Films #2217
Above Excerpt from Son of Frankenstein (1939) Castle Films #1033

ones—I was not possessed by the pangs of nostalgia that my two older friends shared, and was far more concerned with spending what money I had to my name on available Vaughn Bodé collectibles that were absent from my growing collection. During the last hour of the last day, the two were still hemming and hawing over the plastic binder that held the remaining sketches, each hoping to get the dealer to sell them all at a bulk rate. The seller declined, knowing he had already parted with the other pieces for a pittance, leaving my two friends to regret their decision not to splurge for years to come, but cherishing the few they did manage to acquire.

A few years ago, one of the two dealers was forced to part with his original art in order to replace a dead car. I myself was unable to scrape together the asking price but attempted to do so anyway, the seeds of this article having been firmly planted by the offer. I was frustrated to discover a few weeks later that he had sold them in the interim for almost a *third* of his original price tag to another collector who—unlike me—had a *real* job and who also had the forethought to make him a lower offer on the entire lot. Unbowed in my decision to cover Wood's contribution to *Mars Attacks!* in *Trashfiend*, I contacted both the new owner of these sketches as well as the other dealer, whose original Wood artwork hadn't budged from his cluttered yet impressive collection room in the twenty plus years that had passed.

Eager to show off their prized pieces, both conceded to let me scan the originals and reproduce them here in their uncensored glory. Unfortunately, a disastrous computer crash delayed this book, and by the time I was able to hook up with them in order to borrow the artwork, one of them had dumped his on eBay. Luckily, I was only out two of the nine pieces between them, and thankfully my friend who had originally acquired them

in 1981 had in his possession the grisliest, most controversial offerings Wood produced for *Mars Attacks!*

It wasn't until after I had completed most of the work on this piece that I discovered the existence of Darkstar's hard to find *Mars Attacks Portfolio of Roughs*, and pieced together the probability that the publisher was also the dealer looking to unload them at the 1981 expo I attended as a young teen. The one collector—from whom I was unable to borrow the artwork before eBay had claimed it—had tracked down the man responsible for the portfolio in order to verify their authenticity, but I had no luck in getting the dealer turned publisher to respond to my emails for a possible interview.

The gem amongst this original artwork was a finished pen and ink piece that was, more than any other, distinctly Wood. This card depicts a perky young woman caught writhing in the web of a giant spider closing in for the kill, both knee deep in the skeletal remains of its prior meals. Above the crumbling backdrop several Air Force planes rush past, the reader left unaware whether the pilots are privy to the deadly drama below. A beautifully rendered piece of comic art, all but the concept was discarded for Saunders' final product. The card that comes closest to capturing the action—#30, aka 'Trapped!!'—features a more intimate reinterpretation of the attack, with the woman exposing less flesh, the spider more comically grotesque, and the ships that imply a possible rescue nowhere to be found.

With the rougher sketches, it is difficult—if not impossible—to tell which ones were supplied by Wood's otherwise deft hand and which ones by Powell. Some of the ones I've reproduced here may instead be Powell's doing, but the dealer insisted that Wood was responsible for all the pieces purchased by my two friends back in 1981.

Aside from the controversy, *Mars Attacks!* is interesting from a historical perspective in that it marks the death of one trend and the birth of another. By 1962, extraterrestrials and giant insects had lost their foothold as the bogeymen of choice in cinema and comic books, with the return of more traditional monsters in their stead. It also precipitated the interest in more graphic horror fare that swelled through the sixties and burst open like a ripe boil in the seventies. Although *Mars Attacks!* was easily quashed by the backlash of concerned mothers all across the United States, such attempts to hold back the tide of explicit violence depicted in various 'artistic' mediums would lose much of their power in the years to come.

❑ **Wally Wood horror comics & magazine checklist, see page 299**
❑ *Mars Attacks!* **trading cards checklist, see page 298**

NOTES

1 Remember that Herschell Gordon Lewis' groundbreaking exercise in splatter filmmaking, Blood Feast (1963), was released to an unsuspecting public only a year later. The film proved profitable enough for him to continue churning out a new gore film every year or two until, with the market glutted with ultra violent fare, he retired from filmmaking in 1972.

2 According to Len, the title was changed at the last minute because they "felt that a two word title would have more of an impact than a three word title." Without a doubt, Mars Attacks! is a far punchier moniker, but it's interesting that they made such a change when the product was already a proven seller as Attack from Space. In the business where the motto is "If it ain't broke, don't fix it," this is considered as taking a tremendous risk.

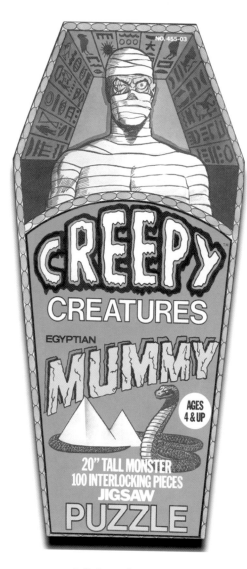

Left Box art for Creepy Creatures: The Mummy Jigsaw Puzzle (1975) H-G Toys, Inc. #455-03
Right Puzzle for Creepy Creatures: The Mummy Jigsaw Puzzle (1975) H-G Toys, Inc. #455-03

ALTHOUGH MOVIES, comics and magazines take up a large part of any young horror fan's life, we all had our share of toys and games, novelties and accoutrements with which to indulge our many macabre interests. Here is a modest potpourri of nifty monster related memorabilia from the sixties and seventies in which to browse, some of which you may have had, or coveted having seen advertisements. If this proves to be your introduction, even better.

Creepy Creatures: The Frankenstein Monster jigsaw puzzle (1975)
H-G Toys, Inc. #455-01 [Long Beach, CA, USA]
Box dimensions: 5¾" x 11½" x 2"
Puzzle dimensions: 9½" x 20" (100 pieces)

Creepy Creatures: Count Dracula jigsaw puzzle (1975)
H-G Toys, Inc. #455-02 [Long Beach, CA, USA]
Box dimensions: 5¾" x 11½" x 2"
Puzzle dimensions: 9½" x 20" (100 pieces)

Creepy Creatures: Egyptian Mummy jigsaw puzzle (1975)
H-G Toys, Inc. #455-03 [Long Beach, CA, USA]
Box dimensions: 5¾" x 11½" x 2"
Puzzle dimensions: 9½" x 20" (100 pieces)

Creepy Creatures: Dr Jekyll & Mr Hyde jigsaw puzzle (1975)
H-G Toys, Inc. #458 [Long Beach, CA, USA]
Box dimensions: 8½" x 17" x 2½"
Puzzle dimensions: 14½" x 36" (100 pieces)

I still remember when, at about the age of six, I caught sight of my first two (and for several decades, my only two) Creepy Creatures jigsaw puzzles at local variety store Wigwam. (The store went under some time in the early eighties, although a Seattle Costume & Display now resides in the same location, which I religiously peruse every October to check out the latest supply of Halloween goodies. Somehow fitting, that.) On one of Wigwam's clearance shelves, scattered with remaindered toys, were two puzzles that came in coffin shaped boxes, one for the Mummy and one for Frankenstein's monster. I begged, I pleaded, and eventually I persuaded my mother to buy them for me, probably with the promise of performing extra chores for the following week. She probably thought that she was getting the better end of the deal, because the clearance puzzles amounted to less than a dollar, but I knew who had really come out on top.

I had numerous monster related jigsaw puzzles as a child, but these were ultimately my favorites. Cool packaging aside—they were *coffins*…how groovy was that!—the monsters displayed a distinctly seventies flavor, for they steered clear of Universal's copyrighted depictions of the classic monsters. Frankenstein's monster eschewed the flattop look for long flowing hair, and resembled a Haitian zombie more than Boris Karloff. The Mummy boasted a single, buggy, bloodshot eye, and didn't bear much resemblance to Karloff either. Alas, in a fit of temporary insanity during my tumultuous teens, when I had tired of collecting monster fare and dumped most of what I had acquired over the years at the local flea market, the puzzles and I parted ways, the pieces worn and their boxes a little worse for wear.

About twenty years later I found myself trying to get back all the crap I had as a kid without putting myself forever in debt, and stumbled across an advert in a toy collector's journal for three Creepy Creatures jigsaw puzzles. Three? Lo and behold, there also existed one of Count Dracula. Although unimpressed by H-G Toys' interpretation—being a rather sad cross between Lugosi and Lee's portrayals—I was ecstatic at the opportunity to own not only the two puzzles I had as a child but also one in the series on which I had never laid eyes. Long story short, I ordered them for an exorbitant amount, and discovered that the dealer was either a shyster or a complete idiot, as the "Near Mint" puzzles were not only missing pieces, it appeared that the boxes had once been used as chew toys by the family pet. I immediately mailed them back and insisted on a full refund, and soon found myself dodging epithets from the seller for the audacity of calling him out. And that was the last I saw of these puzzles until I discovered eBay a few years later.

Awaiting me on the world's online marketplace was yet another surprise: a *fourth* Creepy Creatures jigsaw puzzle. This time out, Jekyll & Hyde got the honors. Even more surprising, it was a double sided puzzle that was *twice* as large as the other three. Within a few months, I had secured all four puzzles between three different sellers. (Although in one case, I managed to get scammed on the Frankenstein puzzle a second time, without the consolation of a refund.) Since then, I have kept my eyes peeled for any others in the series that might exist, but I have only come up with multiples of the four I own. Curiously, the Werewolf—whom I thought would have taken precedent over King Tut and RL Stevenson's poster child for bipolar disorder—is absent from the lineup.

The art on the front and back of each box differ, with the back depicting the completed puzzle itself, sans cut lines. Unfortunately, the artists for the puzzles are not credited, but from the dissimilar styles one can assume that at least two different artists were responsible, if not more. (If

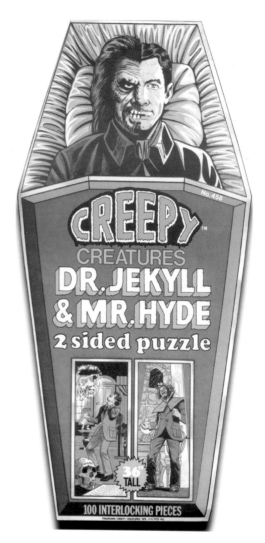

Box art for Creepy Creatures: Dr. Jekyll & Mr. Hyde Jigsaw Puzzle (1975) H-G Toys, Inc. #458

this was a job given to house artists, each piece of art could also be a collaborative effort to varying degrees.)

Although the Creepy Creatures puzzles have become increasingly hard to find, H-G Toys was not a small toy manufacturer by any means. During the seventies, they produced a great many jigsaw puzzles, including ones for such popular television shows as *Godzilla, Planet of the Apes, Shogun Warriors, Space: 1999, Star Trek,* and a

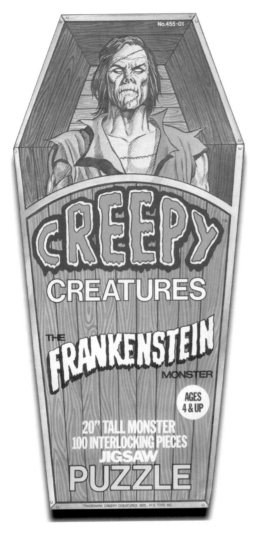

Left Box art for Creepy Creatures: The Frankenstein Monster Jigsaw Puzzle (1975) H-G Toys, Inc. #455-01
Right Puzzle for Creepy Creatures: The Frankenstein Monster Jigsaw Puzzle (1975) H-G Toys, Inc. #455-01

slew of other, non genre programs. So, the chances that there are any more in this set is infinitesimally small, although I would love to be proven wrong.

I have yet to see anything written about these puzzles, or even inclusions in any toy or monster collector's guides. I don't recall seeing any adverts for them in magazines, so they probably had a fairly limited release that didn't warrant a big push outside of modest floor displays in retail outlets.

Curious though is the date they were issued. All the puzzles are marked 1974 on the lower edge of the back of the box, but 1975 on the lower flap, with the exception of Dr Jekyll & Mr Hyde, which is only marked 1975. Copies of these puzzles in mid to high grade condition routinely sell for ten to twenty dollars on eBay, although I've seen some online dealers try to get as much as fifty for lesser copies, so buyer beware. Although the smaller size puzzles are a little easier to find, there doesn't seem to be any more of a demand for the larger one, which may have something to do with the popularity of the subjects. Because of the boxes' unique but flimsy construction, they are easily crushed and the flaps often creased and torn, but ultimately they are worth owning in whatever shape one can find them in.

Monsters, Ghouls & Assorted Creeps Stationery Pad (1965)
Paula #ASP-108 [Cincinnati, OH, USA] 59¢
Notepad dimensions: 5½" x 9¼" (24 sheets)

This odd little piece I recently discovered while rummaging through the disheveled stock of a local used magazine store, having never seen one before or since. (Alas, I have no trips down memory lane to share about this piece... much to the reader's chagrin, I'm sure.) Keeping true to the popularity of *monstres drôles* in the mid sixties, this notepad includes twenty four sheets displaying twelve different headers or borders that feature various ghouls accompanied by humorous one-liners. Most of the illustrations are retouched b&w photographs presented in two tone color.

Unfortunately, the pad I acquired is missing seven sheets, and one of the sheets bears an undelivered note to a teacher about Bobby's tardy homework due to his inability to comprehend the material. Worse, of the remaining sheets, both copies of one particular design are missing, so I only know what eleven of the twelve designs look like. Oh, well, it only cost me a dollar... which is funny in that I paid forty one cents above the suggested retail price for an incomplete, used pad of paper. Collectors are funny people, indeed.

After numerous online searches, I have failed to find an upgrade, and have been unable to track down any information concerning the production company, which simply went by the name of Paula. Furthermore, the sheets themselves bear a

Cover art for Monsters, Ghouls & Assorted Creeps Stationary Pad (1965) Paula #ASP-108

copyright date of 1964, whereas the cover states 1965. The suggested retail price of fifty nine cents seems to me a bit pricey for the mid sixties, so it is quite possible that Paula was a fairly small outfit. But, even if this had extensive distribution, it remains one of the most ephemeral or disposable pieces in my collection, so chances of me locating a high grade replacement any time soon is a classic case of wishful thinking.

Famous Monsters buttons (1963)
Elwar, Ltd #9143 [New York, NY, USA]
Pinback dimensions: 1" x 1" (6 pieces)
Label dimensions: 4" x 4¾"

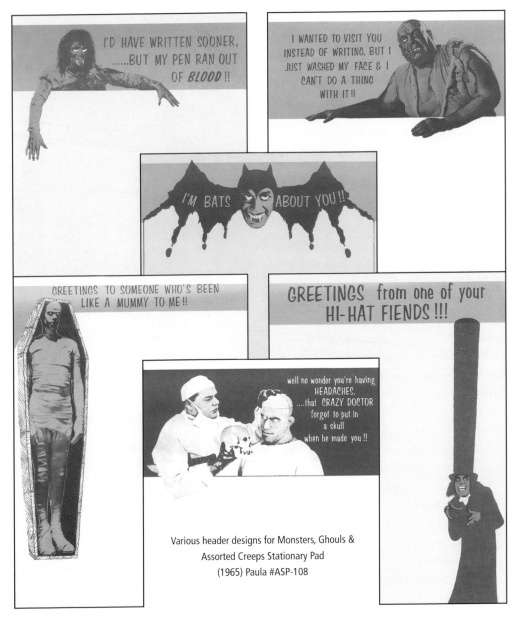

Various header designs for Monsters, Ghouls &
Assorted Creeps Stationary Pad
(1965) Paula #ASP-108

What self respecting Universal Monster fan
could resist such groovy pinbacks? Originally
sold through—you guessed right—the Captain
Company adverts in the back pages of *Famous
Monsters of Filmland*, these metal buttons could
also be obtained from gumball style vending machines. Each bears a desaturated painted image of
Universal's more popular monsters against a red

or yellow backdrop, namely Lon Chaney's The
Phantom (of the Opera), Lon Chaney Jr's The
Mummy and Wolfman, Bela Lugosi's Dracula,
Glenn Strange's Frankenstein (Monster), and
The Creature (from the Black Lagoon).

I have yet to determine who was responsible
for the painted artwork that appears on these
pinbacks. It doesn't appear to be the handiwork of

SLEEPLESS IN SEATTLE: UP ALL NIGHT WITH NIGHTMARE THEATRE

Warning: Not recommended for those with an aversion to effusive sentimentality and nostalgia

FOR MOST horror fans in the thirty something age bracket and older, our earliest exposures to monster movies on late night television were introduced by a makeup laden host or hostess with a penchant for debilitating puns. If you were a child of the fifties, you may have been exposed to the ample charms of Morticia Addams knock-off Vampira; an adolescent in the eighties would have been weaned on her valley bred doppelganger Elvira. If you were lucky enough to have been a sixties baby boomer, the heyday of horror hosts gave us the timeless likes of Dr Morgus, Ghoulardi and—last but not least—Zacherley, who even lent his marketable persona to numerous books and records over the years. At least one station in every major city can lay claim to a weekly creature feature program with a resident dime store ghoul as the viewer's tour guide in years past, and Seattle was no exception.

As a young boy in the seventies, I was lucky enough to have witnessed Washington's seminal horror host. He was called simply 'The Count,' and he was the mascot for the similarly generic sounding *Nightmare Theatre*.[1] From the time I learned to sneak out of bed, until the show went off the air a few years later, I watched the program religiously. It was specifically this show that

taught me to read by the age of four, and it was the TV guide that took the stead of *Dick & Jane* for yours truly. My mother—having grown tired of me constantly asking her what was playing on television—promised me that if I learned to read the TV guide by myself, I could watch anything I wanted, any time, day or night.

Before long, I could recognize the telltale genre label of 'Thriller' and 'Sci fi' that accompanied every monster movie listed therein, and within a year I had grasped all the basics of the written word. More importantly, I had discovered a curious event. Every Friday night, at 11:30 (unless pre-empted by a far less interesting movie of the week), Channel 7 would show not one horror film, but *two*, back to back. My parents attempted to recant their promise of "any time, day or night" but they soon relented; it was futile. Even when they said no, I could be found slinking out of my bed after they turned in for the night, gluing myself to the television set in the living room, the sound turned down to almost inaudible, staring glassy eyed at the flickering glass teat into the wee hours of the morning.

There was more to the viewing experience than three to four hours of monster mayhem. Although I made every attempt to see each and every horror flick shown on the five stations broadcast in our area, regardless of how many times I may have already seen them, this was different. *Nightmare Theatre* was an event, a weekly ritual that may have contributed to my burgeoning obsessive compulsive behavior. The show was hosted by a vampire, and a funny one at that. (Okay, so even at that age I knew The Count wasn't the real McCoy, but nonetheless it was fun to pretend he was.) Having been shot live on video, he seemed so much more real than the ghouls in the old scratchy b&w films he gleefully introduced to us.

The show opened with the soon familiar *Nightmare Theatre* logo, shown against a mini-

Separated at birth? Not quite, but the hair and teeth are sure to throw many people off.
Promotional photos for Jonathan Frid as Barnabas Collins (**left**) and Joe Towey as The Count (**right**)
Dan Curtis Productions and KIRO-TV Productions, respectively.

ature old house exterior surrounded by lolling mist. As the camera approached, the scene dissolved into a painted set piece of a stone wall with a single paneless window, lit by several candles. The scene was accompanied by a deep sepulcher-like voiceover, spooky music and canned sound effects (the latter of which were culled from the title track on *Walt Disney's Chilling, Thrilling Sounds of the Haunted House*). A coffin sat center stage, its lid slowly opened by unseen hands (in actuality a wire suspended from a pulley in the lighting grid). Inside the casket resided a skeleton, which—through the cinematic magic of a dissolve fade—became The Count. The pasty faced ghoul would pull himself up with his white gloved hands, a familiar, wonderfully grating laugh escaping his lips. Show time!

The Count bore as much resemblance to *Dark Shadows'* Barnabas Collins as he did to a cookie-cutter Dracula (which probably only con-

tributed to my affinity for the host). Although spared the obligatory widow's peak, he did wield a Bela Lugosi inspired Transylvanian accent, almost as clumsily as he handled everything else (all intentional, I might add). Rarely frightened by the films in which I reveled, his presence only reinforced the notion that monster movies were indeed *fun*.

Occasionally, I was allowed to have sleepovers on Friday, or would stay the night at another friend's house, but never would I miss *Nightmare Theatre*, with my guests usually falling asleep before the opening credits of the second feature scrolled across the screen. Wrapped up in my sleeping bag, I would watch in rapt attention until The Count made his melodramatic exit at the close of the show. Not knowing if they would ever re-run a film (remember, this was in the days before we were blessed with the luxury known as VCRs), I would commit every frame of film seeing The Count on a television commercial featuring Cal Worthington, the colorful head of a local car dealership who was known for his 'dog' Spot—actually some large, exotic, usually drugged animal on loan for the ad spots—and for such hijinks as smashing in car windows with a sledgehammer. Luckily for us animal lovers, he never combined the two gimmicks.)

October was tough, especially in the days leading up to Halloween, as I was incessantly pining for the days when I would curl up in front of the television on Friday nights, comforted by the flickering images that lulled me into a dazed stupor. I wound up subjecting my new roommate to a slew of my own late night double features. Unfortunately, having sold off the bulk of my video collection that summer, I had to make do with a great many films that were never shown on *Nightmare Theatre*. Alas, as much as I adore all things sixties and seventies, the films from that era could never take the place of those b&w wonders that featured the likes of Boris Karloff, Bela Lugosi and Lon Chaney Jr.

Things were coming to a head. The first draft of my book was nearing a state of completion, and I still hadn't contacted KIRO. Granted, I had been bogged down with life's hurdles since I accepted this undertaking, but I was starting to get the feeling that there was something more to my reluctance, something subconscious. Was I afraid that KIRO, my last shot of cracking the mystery of *Nightmare Theatre*, would prove fruitless and thus leave me with nowhere else to turn? Or was I afraid that I would actually find many of the answers that I sought, thus bringing an end to my quest and leaving me again with only hazy recollections? Regardless, it was time to bring this chapter to a close, even if the story remained open ended.

The closing months of 2004 were particularly taxing, as my financial situation worsened.

Joe Towey at the helms of The J.P. Patches Show (circa 1970s) City Dump Productions

The desire to retreat into a childhood that spoke of simpler times increased, but time and means were at a minimum. I made it through the holidays, undoubtedly worse for wear; one of my New Year's resolutions was to wrap up the *Nightmare Theatre* project, to bring it to something of a conclusion. A full year had passed since I began working on the piece you are now reading, a year that could be best summed up by the analogy of a drunk stumbling in a dark alley looking for a pot to piss in. So, with nowhere else to turn, I telephoned KIRO.

I was immediately put at ease by the woman who answered my call. When I mentioned what show it was I was writing about, she admitted, "Oh, my God, I remember that show!" Suddenly, her voice had that distinct ring of nostalgia that I had come to expect from people who recalled the show with fond sentiments. She flipped through her Rolodex trying to find someone who may have worked at KIRO during the show's run, and transferred me to someone's voicemail. I left a short, stuttering message (have I mentioned just how much I hate answering machines?) and called her back. She took another look through her list of personnel and came up with another name. Before she transferred me a second time, I asked if there was anyone in archives who could help me out with the basics. Unfortunately, it turned out that archives dealt primarily with news stories and not station history; furthermore, she said that the person in charge of that department was probably still in diapers when *Nightmare Theatre* went off the air, thus clueless as to what I was talking about. Unfortunately, the second transfer yielded a constant ring, but no voicemail.

The chance the first gentleman would get back to me was slim; heck, if he could actually translate my garbled message into English, it would be a miracle. Calling back the receptionist at KIRO a third time in one day would probably be tantamount to harassment, so I thought it best to wait at least twenty four hours. In the meantime, I decided to scour my files, having belatedly remembered that Wedes had given me a list of possible contacts at KIRO earlier the previous year. Although things were looking grim, I had not given up hope, stubborn bastard that I am.

I couldn't leave well enough alone. This chapter wouldn't see print for at least a year, and would only resonate with a handful of people when it did, so the thought that I had done little to extricate my childhood hero from the pages of local history weighed heavy on me. (Okay, so maybe I wasn't nearly as burdened by the guilt as I make out, but I was at the very least thoroughly annoyed.) It was then I decided to follow the road traveled by so many other desperate fans pining for a lost childhood: I decided to create a webpage in honor of the influential program. Instead of a page, I wound up laying out an entire site toenailed to my online storefront for my self publishing endeavors. I had the memory to accommodate it, and it would take little effort to hobble together something modest and functional.

Months passed with nary a peep, my life still a veritable mess, but then out of the proverbial blue in May of 2005 came an email from Dave Drui,

morning host and production director for AM 820 KGNW out of Seattle. His letter started, "Stumbled upon your website for *Nightmare Theatre* and it seemed like you needed some sources to find out the inside story. I'm one. I worked on the show." Without hesitation, I secured my third interview for this piece, and by far the most promising of the lot. From this, I was able to verify exactly who worked on the program, at least during the seventies. With a few more leads at my disposal, I attempted to resume my quest, having taken something of another forced sabbatical in the months previous.

Unfortunately, just as I was attempting to pick up where I had left off, I found deadlines for the book sneaking up on me, forcing me to bring the article to something akin to closure in order to supply a very patient publisher with copy. By July, I was still bogged down with *Trashfiend*, the book having taken on a girth I hadn't expected. My finances were still a mess, especially in light of my living and breathing the book for the best part of a month without any means to secure an income. I was tired with a capital T, but for the first time since I had made my decision to unearth The Count, I was hopeful.

Things were finally falling into place, yet I still could not shake the feelings of loss every time I was confronted with the subject of *Nightmare Theatre*. Each time I came across a reference to a film that I had caught on Channel 7 late one Friday night for the first time, I found myself pining for the experience. I could still watch *The Mole People* and *Invasion of the Saucer Men* back to back and enjoy myself immensely, but I could never recreate the moment when these films first revealed themselves to me, courtesy of The Count.

At this point in my life, I am lucky in that I have lost very few loved ones, but I have strong memories of these people, and the photographs with which to spark them. For The Count, I have but a few pictures that stir within me some very vague, mostly fragmented recollections. Most everything else from my childhood that I cherished—my books and comics, the games and jigsaw puzzles, even the Avon monster soap dish and *The Lost World Monster Maker* from Mattel—I know I will eventually replace. Save for the memories of slogging through chores and schoolwork, the end of each week punctuated by an eagerly anticipated visit from The Count, *Nightmare Theatre* is something that is forever lost.

Postscript

AS I HAMMER OUT this last minute addendum, I am still recovering from a devastating computer crash, one that consumed most of this book in one fell swoop only weeks before I was to have the final drafts and rough layouts to the publisher. In a little over three months, I have pieced together, and—in many cases—completely rewritten the book from hard copy notes and fragments rescued from restored cache files. (What happened to my art files—some of which were irreplaceable in the time allotted me—is a horror story in itself.) At one point, I was certain that *Trashfiend* was lost, which would have made the book's already depressing closing statements eerily apropos. But, unable to let it all end on such a nihilistic note, I pressed on.

I was barely a week away from submitting the final draft of the book (this time, copies of everything have been saved on a secondary hard drive) when I received two unexpected emails within days of one another. The first was from a man by the name of…Joe Towey. Had this been one of the low rent horror movies reviewed within these pages, it would have been sent by the restless spirit of a childhood idol telling me that the book was cursed for reasons beyond my comprehen-

sion and that I should abandon the project before even more ill befell my person and property. In lieu of a warning from beyond the grave, though, was a message from his grandson, stating, "I just found the site and think that it is really cool that you are doing that, though it is kind of weird to see a site about my grampa." He also offered whatever assistance he could in the way of stories and art, which gave me hope that this chapter wouldn't end on such a sour note. (Unfortunately, the chance that Joe the younger would be able to share any first person recollection was, well, infinitesimal, since he was born within a year of his grandfather's passing.)

The second email was from one Derik Loso, a stage manager at KIRO who said he "might be able to help with a little bit of information and perhaps some visual material concerning Joe Towey as The Count." After I gladly accepted his help, he offered me a tour of the station as well as an opportunity to speak with several coworkers who had worked alongside Joe. He also mentioned access to some memorabilia and some video clips. Video clips? They had video clips? I rushed him a response, explaining that I would get back to him once I secured a ride to the studio. (Alas, I don't drive, otherwise I would have been down there the following day if it were at all possible.)

Unfortunately, both of these offers came much too close to an already taxed deadline, which meant… a sequel? I wasn't about to let these opportunities slip through the cracks, even if it meant I would be branded as a tease. I would do everything in my power to make sure this book was a success… if only so I could continue to tell the story of a man and his late night television program, both of which may be the reasons I wrote this book to begin with.

All I can say is… stay tuned for more after these commercial messages.

NOTES

1 Apparently, The Count was not the first; this title went to Warren Reed & Frankie, who hosted a late night Seattle show in the fifties. During the seventies, The Count had some competition, supplied by Robert 'Dr ZinGRR' Smith, who had his own program on Channel 13 from 1971 to 1976. As a child, I never caught ZinGRR's exploits, because where I lived had limited reception, and 13's signal would not reach us for another few years.

2 Having owned these films now since the day they were released on tape, I still attempt to relive the experience once a year without fail, curled up on the couch with a ready bowl of Boo Berry, Count Chocula or Frankenberry in my lap. (Occasionally, an unwary friend is subjected to the experience as well, but they never come back for seconds the following year when invited. Maybe they just don't like General Mills monster cereals, I don't know.) Unfortunately, the repeated double bills never hold up to the first time; not because I'm thirty years older and have become jaded to the films' charms, but because The Count isn't there to, well, interrupt the proceedings with a bad joke or accidentally slam a coffin lid on his gloved fingers.

3 The extended date rang true, at least as far as the seventies was concerned. I thought I had watched Nightmare Theatre for more than the three plus years that the 1968–75 airing didn't account for—with or without The Count—but chalked it up to a young child's faulty memory.

4 Sci fi Theatre, which was usually aired between twelve and two in the afternoon, has had a major impact on my viewing experience as an adult. To this day, I can only watch vintage Godzilla films and Italian sci fi from the sixties during the daylight hours, lest I fall asleep midway. Not pertinent to anything, this endnote—like several of the others—is included only for those desperate readers who for whatever sick reason can't get enough of my maudlin reminiscences. Be assured I've done my best to accommodate you, you poor bastards.

5 I later received from another fan an MP3 struck from an audiotape recording he had made of the show back in 1979. Although the opening monologue was missing, the existing bits mention the film being shown was Frankenstein: The True Story (1973); after a quick jaunt to the library, I was able to verify that this special aired October 31, 1979, at 11:30 on Channel 7. And, yes, I myself missed The Count's return—and ultimately final—television appearance. With luck, the rest of the footage not shown on JP Patches Memories was also spared.

Anyone interested in further plumbing the depths of all that is Nightmare Theatre, including full program schedules and other fan reminisces, feel free to check out my webpage at www.nightmaretheatrenw.net.

All images pertaining to Nightmare Theatre and The JP Patches Show are copyrighted by KIRO-TV Productions and/or City Dump Productions.

In Memory of Joe "The Count" Towey (d. April 9, 1989)

out of it. The bit started with crew members, and then the crew started grabbing people from down the hall—radio folks, office staff, anyone they could find in the building that night. Then finally The Count emerges from the coffin and says "Wow, that was a wild party!" The opening ran about ten minutes. It was hysterical! KIRO management didn't think so. Lloyd Cooney, the president of KIRO, happened to be watching that night and blew his stack. He didn't understand that no one tuned in to *Nightmare Theatre* to see the funky old b&w Vincent Price movies we'd all seen over and over again, but viewers' attraction to the show was the funny opens, mid breaks and closes! Lloyd thought that long drawn out open was just too much and it was off the air the following week.

Was this in 1975?

You tell me. Sounds about right, though.

*Didn't the program continue as **Nightmare Theatre** but without Joe Towey's wraparound for a while? Were you involved with the one-off Halloween special featuring The Count and an all too familiar **Nightmare Theatre** backdrop that was aired 1978? If so, how did it come about, considering KIRO's lack of enthusiasm for the program?*

Seems to me that sounds right. Yeah, just the movies without Joe for a while, since the sales team had already sold it, and KIRO was and *is* never one to give up money! Don't know anything about the special unfortunately. I was working mornings on *The JP Patches Show* by then. The night crew probably put that together.

*When and how did you become involved with **The JP Patches Show**?*

Usually you had to wait for someone to quit or die to move into a full time position at KIRO, but in 1977 a decision was made to expand. Since KIRO had two studios—one with the sets for the everyday live shows like *JP* and the news programs, the other empty—KIRO thought they could make more money by having an on air live crew in Studio A and one that just produced commercials all day in Studio B. Rick Jones, who had been the floor director for the clown show forever, wanted a break and opted to work in commercials so I was promoted to full time morning floor director. I worked alone until after the clown show, and Bob Newman got out of his makeup and came on the crew as our second Studio A floor director. He only worked Monday, Wednesday and Friday as *JP* was a second banana at that time, 1977–78 (a money saving measure by KIRO). Sometimes another floor director from Studio B came over to help, Sharon Leimbacher (now Howard), when she didn't have a production to set up for. Joe decided this would be a good way for me to have more input into the show by adding the second floor director... more flexibility for me handling the props, throwing pies, coming up with plot ideas, and even occasionally acting on the show. Funny thing, legally Joe couldn't request me to come on as an actor because then KIRO would have to pay me according to my AFTRA contract, but if 'I' suggested it and volunteered to appear it was no problem and KIRO didn't lose any money. I remember begging for money out of the budget to buy shaving cream for the pies we threw. Sometimes I wouldn't bother and just bought the Barbasol myself.

*Do you remember some of the roles you played on **The JP Patches Show**?*

The first one I just adlibbed into a bit JP was doing with Miss Smith (Newman), where she was telling him a joke about a frog. Since we had a frog on the show named Morgan who was nothing more than a hand puppet that Bob operated and provided the voice for, I just shoved him on my hand, pushed him in camera view, imitated Bob's voice and said to the audience "Say, I didn't like that very much!" They both cracked up. They'd been working with just the two of them for so long it was a bit disorienting having a third cog on the show again, but that opened the door for me to do other bits, as Ggoorrsstt the friendly Frpl, as Joe Cannelloni the Green Grocer, as Mayor Royer, and finally in the Thanksgiving special as a Darth Vader knock-off, Y from the Planet Z. I played it for comedy and instead of sounding deep and scary like James Earl Jones I used a voice like Don Adams doing Maxwell Smart.

On The JP Patches Show, Towey would make occasional guest appearances; did anyone from Wedes' program ever show up in front of the camera on Nightmare Theatre, or was it pretty much a one-vampire show?

No. Since we taped at night, Joe was the only talent there, although I would occasionally lend a hand as a monster at the door. Once I was a severed hand inside a box under Joe's arm that suddenly sprang to life and choked him during an open; I was actually crouching underneath Joe's cape behind him and there was a hole cut in the end of the shoebox to slip my hand through. I was doing all kinds of things back there to make Joe break up while we were taping—that was always the goal—but he never did.

Did The Count ever appear on The JP Patches Show for cross promotion? Can you recall any appearances he made as The Count outside of the show?

I know that Joe made some personal appearances with JP and by himself, especially around Halloween, but on the clown show we had our own cast of evil nemeses, all played by Bob New-

man, like Boris S Wart, the second meanest man in the world, and the dreaded witch Zenobia who would materialize every year around Halloween.

Besides the clip that appears on the JP Patches Memories video compilation, do you know of any Nightmare Theatre footage that has survived?

Unfortunately, due to the high cost of videotape in those days (it was all done on huge reels of two inch tape, not VHS), there's none of that stuff left as far as I know. If anyone would have any of it, Mike Speten is your best bet. He ran the tape machine and is the reason *The JP Patches Show* has any archive clips available at all, because he started taping some on old two inch videotape that was about to be discarded.

It has been rumored that KIRO-TV had the largest collection of horror films in the Pacific Northwest. Was this true, as far as you know? Who chose the films to be aired?

I'm not sure about that. Dick Jacoby was the film vault guy, who doesn't work there anymore.

How do you best remember Joe Towey?

My last day at KIRO Joe, who normally only worked mornings, stayed until the very end of my shift and walked me out to the door at six pm. Not knowing what to say as we parted, I held out my hand to him and said, "Well, it was great working with you". He wouldn't shake my hand and was actually offended! He told me, "You don't know if we'll work together again or not... don't say that... don't say 'it was great working with you' like it's all over! Just don't say that!" Sure enough, six months after I moved to Los Angeles, California, I got a call from KIRO and they flew me back and I was once again working with Joe—and JP and Gertrude—as an actor this time on a *JP Patches* Thanksgiving Special.

What are your fondest memories of working on Nightmare Theatre?

It was always a gas the one night a month we did the taping. Lots of fun playing around with the different ideas for the bits Joe would do. Since it was taped we took a lot of liberties with not-so-airable outtakes before we taped the one we actually aired. Some were pretty raunchy…but pretty hysterical, though. Like the hand through the shoebox routine I explained above. Before we did the actual take where I slowly reach up and strangle The Count, I couldn't resist and elevated my hand slowly with just the middle finger extended. Joe didn't miss a beat and kept up his Transylvanian patter by inserting "…and da scary movies we haff for you tonight [my gesture] and the letters vee are going to get from da viewers… and vee will be off the air! I can see it… it vill be the end of my career!" I've never laughed so hard!

You made the offer of regaling me with more Nightmare Theatre anecdotes when you first contacted me through my website, so now I'm holding you to it. For the benefit of us fans who are desperately trying to relive these years, fire away!

There was another one that didn't make the air, but it should have. Joe was going to surprise the viewers; instead of being inside the coffin he would be behind it, and as we're holding on the usual side shot of the box waiting for him to emerge he would suddenly slam down the lid from behind. Remember, the goal was to get Joe and try to make him break—character, that is, and get him to crack up laughing—so I sneaked a bucket of water on the set behind a camera and just as the lid of the coffin slammed down revealing The Count behind, I was there immediately dowsing him with the full bucket of water. It was an almost instantaneous "SLAM, WOOSH!", but again Joe never missed a beat. He just kept

on with his patter and inserted "…and the people who work on this show—or should I say *used* to work on this show—are going to pay, boy are they going to pay!"

And did he ever get or try to get payback for all the tricks the cast and crew pulled on him over the years?

He didn't, but Bob Newman did. Even though I got Joe once with the water, Newman paid me back for the buckets and buckets I'd dowsed him with over the years on the clown show. When JP went on vacation, Bob would host the show alone—an hour a day for two weeks with no one to play off of—so it got a little tedious at times. I tried to break in with a little humor by knocking at the door, he'd open it and I'd pummel him with a bucket of water.

There was one day in particular. There were all the little stuffed creatures that JP had around the set that issued nothing more than a giggle or a sound effect supplied from the audio man's booth, and that day they all had miniature buckets full of water, and over the course of the hour they all hit Newman with (what amounted to) gallons and gallons of water. Bob got so that he could hardly answer the knock at the door he was laughing so much. Well, he got me back. My last day on the show, JP had come to say goodbye and, sure enough, as I was leaving, Newman was waiting outside the door with a full bucket of you know what and he soaked me from head to toe. The only difference was that, after the show, Bob always had a change of dry clothes to get into. I didn't. I had to work the rest of my eight hour shift soaking wet. Thanks Newman! But it sure was a blast!

What was the first horror film you saw as a child? What kind of impression did it leave on you?

Some mom in the neighborhood took a bunch of us kids to the movie theatre in Redmond one summer day to see *Billy Rose's Jumbo* (1962) with Doris Day and Jimmy Durante. Little did she know there was a terrific horror flick preceding it on the double bill. It involved knights, witches, swamps, and was excellently done... it gave me nightmares for years! Wish I could remember the name of it.

I also remember Saturday afternoons watching horror flicks on TV... maybe it was Channel 7. My favorite was a giant ant film—not *Them!* (1954)—with no name stars, fake looking ant puppets and really bad acting. Real camp stuff. The best scene was where expert scientists are called out to check out the big marks in the sand caused by these creatures. Nothing special, just some holes in the ground. After a grueling inspection, one guy in a lab coat looks up from a hole and says very seriously, "There's only *one* thing this could be... giant ants!" I don't remember the name of the film, but it was something like *Attack of the Giant Ants*, although I could be getting the title mixed up with my second favorite awful horror flick of the time, *Attack of the Crab Monsters* (1957).

Having probably sat through many of the films aired by Nightmare Theatre, *what do you see as the most noticeable differences between modern day horror fare and those shown on the program?*

So much of the old films relied on your imagination; they were much scarier for that reason. I don't even watch the modern slasher films just for that reason.

I don't blame you. Although I have no problem with gore, the older films are so much more atmospheric and evocative. Are there any modern horror films you've seen you do like?

I wouldn't say horror films are my favorite, but rather suspense thrillers, classics like *Rear Window* (1954), *Psycho* (1960) and even *Jaws* (1975). My favorite actual horror flick was *The Abominable Dr Phibes* (1971) with Vincent Price. I remember liking that one a lot in high school. I've just ordered it on DVD; I hope it holds up over the years.

In closing, what do you want the epitaph on your tombstone to read?

What is this, *Inside the Actor's Studio?* Okay, how about: "Here lies Dave Drui...who used to work with Joe Towey."

Appendix

Aaron 'Pat' Boyette (1923–2000)
aka Alexander Barnes,
Bruce Lovelace, Sam Swell

selected horror comics checklist
(1966–79)

BARON WEIRWULF'S HAUNTED LIBRARY see
    HAUNTED

BEYOND THE GRAVE
    (1975–76) [Charlton Comics]
v1#1 (Jul 1975) 25¢

CREEPY
    (1964–83) [Warren Publishing]
#18 (Jan 1968) 40¢
#22 (Aug 1968) 40¢
#33 (Jun 1970) 50¢
#35 (Sep 1970) 50¢
#37 (Jan 1971) 60¢
#39 (May 1971) 60¢
#47 (Sep 1972) 75¢
1971 Annual (1970) 60¢

CREEPY THINGS
    (1975–76) [Charlton Comics]
v2#6 (Jun 1976) 30¢

EERIE
    (1965–83) [Warren Publishing]
#15 (Jun 1968) 40¢
#28 (Jul 1970) 50¢
#30 (Nov 1970) 60¢
#33 (May 1971) 60¢

GHOST MANOR first series
    (1968–71) [Charlton Comics]
    Becomes GHOSTLY HAUNTS with v1#20
v1#13 (Jul 1970) 15¢
v1#16 (Jan 1971) 15¢
v1#17 (Mar 1971) 15¢
v1#19 (Jul 1971) 15¢

GHOST MANOR second series
    (1971–84) [Charlton Comics]
    Cover title VISIT GHOST MANOR
v1#1 (Oct 1971) 20¢
v1#2 (Dec 1971) 20¢
v3#12 (Jun 1973) 20¢
v3#14 (Sep 1973) 20¢
v3#16 (Dec 1973) 20¢
v5#24 (Jul 1975) 25¢
v5#25 (Sep 1975) 25¢
v5#26 (Nov 1975) 25¢
v6#29 (Jun 1976) 30¢
v6#30 (Aug 1976) 30¢
v6#31 (Oct 1976) 30¢
v9#43 (Jun 1979) 40¢

GHOSTLY HAUNTS
    (1971–78) [Charlton Comics]
    Formerly GHOST MANOR (1968–71) first series
v4#22 (Jan 1972) 20¢
v4#24 (Apr 1972) 20¢
v4#26 (Aug 1972) 20¢
v5#32 (May 1973) 20¢
v5#33 (Jul 1973) 20¢
v7#43 (Mar 1975) 25¢
v8#52 (Oct 1976) 30¢

GHOSTLY TALES
    (1966–84) [Charlton Comics]
    Cover title GHOSTLY TALES FROM THE
    HAUNTED HOUSE
v2#58 (Nov 1966) 12¢
v3#59 (Jan 1967) 12¢
v3#60 (Mar 1967) 12¢
v3#61 (Jun 1967) 12¢
v3#62 (Aug 1967) 12¢
v3#63 (Oct 1967) 12¢
v4#65 (Feb 1968) 12¢
v4#66 (May 1968) 12¢
v4#67 (Jul 1968) 12¢
v4#68 (Sep 1968) 12¢
v4#70 (Nov 1968) 12¢
v4#72 (Mar 1969) 12¢
v4#73 (May 1969) 12¢
v4#75 (Sep 1969) 15¢
v5#80 (Jun 1970) 15¢
v5#81 (Aug 1970) 15¢
v5#82 (Oct 1970) 15¢
v5#83 (Dec 1970) 15¢

Left Ghost Manor V6#30 (August 1976) Charlton Comics
Right Haunted V2#9 (December 1972) Charlton Comics

v6#84 (Feb 1971) 15¢
v6#85 (Apr 1971) 15¢
v6#86 (Jun 1971) 15¢
v6#88 (Sep 1971) 15¢
v6#89 (Oct 1971) 20¢
v6#90 (Nov 1971) 20¢
v7#94 (Apr 1972) 20¢
v8#104 (May 1973) 20¢
v8#105 (Jul 1973) 20¢
v8#106 (Aug 1973) 20¢
v9#112 (Dec 1974) 25¢
v10#114 (Apr 1975) 25¢
v13#127 (Jan 1978) 35¢
v13#130 (May 1978) 35¢
v13#132 (Oct 1978) 35¢
v14#137 (Aug 1979) 40¢

GHOSTLY TALES FROM THE HAUNTED HOUSE
    see GHOSTLY TALES

HAUNTED
    (1971–84) [Charlton Comics]
    Cover title BARON WEIRWULF'S HAUNTED
    LIBRARY with v5#21
v1#2 (Nov 1971) 20¢

v2#4 (Feb 1972) 20¢
v2#7 (Aug 1972) 20¢
v2#8 (Oct 1972) 20¢
v2#9 (Dec 1972) 20¢
v3#13 (Jul 1973) 20¢
v3#14 (Sep 1973) 20¢
v4#17 (Jul 1974) 20¢
v4#19 (Dec 1974) 25¢
v5#21 (Apr 1975) 25¢
v6#28 (Jul 1976) 30¢
v8#37 (Jul 1978) 35¢
v9#41 (Mar 1979) 40¢
v9#43 (Jul 1979) 40¢

HAUNTED LOVE
    (1973–75) [Charlton Comics]
v3#7 (Jan 1975) 25¢
v3#9 (May 1975) 25¢
v3#10 (Jun 1975) 25¢

THE MANY GHOSTS OF DOCTOR GRAVES
    (1967–82) [Charlton Comics]
v1#1 (May 1967) 12¢
v1#2 (Jul 1967) 12¢
v1#3 (Sep 1967) 12¢

Man-Thing spot illustration by Pat Broderick

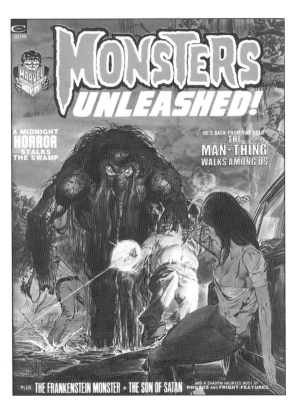

Okay, so you tell me what's really on Manny's mind?
Cover art by Neal Adams for Monsters Unleashed! V1#3
(November 1973) Marvel Comics Group

PASKO, MARTIN (1953–)
+ *Monsters Unleashed!* 2–4

PEARSON, KIT
+ *Monsters Unleashed!* 3
+ *Tales of the Zombie* 1

PENALVA, JORDI
+ *Dracula Lives!* 2

PEREZ, GEORGE (1954–)
+ *Marvel Preview* 12

PERLIN, DON (1929–)
+ *Monsters Unleashed!* 4, 9, Annual 1

PLOOG, MICHAEL 'MIKE' (1942–)
+ *Dracula Lives!* 4
+ *Marvel Preview* 8
+ *Monsters Unleashed!* 6

PLUNKETT, SANDY
+ *Marvel Preview* 8

POLIDORI, DR JOHN WILLIAM (1795–1821)
+ *Vampire Tales* 1

REDONDO, VIRGILIO 'VIRGIL'
+ *Dracula Lives!* 13
+ *Tales of the Zombie* 9–10

REESE, RALPH
+ *The Haunt of Horror* 1
+ *The Legion of Monsters* 1
+ *Masters of Terror* 1–2
+ *Monsters Unleashed!* 1–2
+ *Tales of the Zombie* 2, Annual 1
+ *Vampire Tales* 9

REINMAN, PAUL (1910–)
+ *Vampire Tales* 1, 3–4

RIVAL, RICO
+ *Marvel Preview* 3
+ *Monsters of the Movies* 6
+ *Monsters Unleashed!* 11

ROBBINS, FRANK (1917–)
+ *Dracula Lives!* 9

ROBINSON, CHARLES 'CHUCK'
+ *Tales of the Zombie* 2, Annual 1

ROMERO, ENRIQUE BADIA (1930–)
+ *The Haunt of Horror* 2, 4
+ *Tales of the Zombie* 3, Annual 1

ROMITA, JOHN, SR. (1930–)
+ *Vampire Tales* 2

ROSEN, HY (1923–)
+ *Monsters Unleashed!* 6

ROYER, MICHAEL 'MIKE'
+ *Monsters of the Movies* 4

SATIAN, AL
+ *Monsters of the Movies* 2, 4, 6

SEVERIN, MARIE
+ *Marvel Preview* 8
+ *Masters of Terror* 1

SHORES, SYDNEY 'SYD' (1916–73)
+ *Dracula Lives!* 2–3, Annual 1
+ *The Haunt of Horror* 4
+ *Monsters of the Movies* 2
+ *Monsters Unleashed!* 1–2, 4
+ *Tales of the Zombie* 1, 5, Annual 1

46 Blast Off for Mars
47 Earth Bombs Mars
48 Earthmen Land on Mars
49 The Earthmen Charge
50 Smashing the Enemy
51 Crushing the Martians
52 Giant Robot
53 Martian City in Ruins
54 Mars Explodes
55 Checklist

Mars Attacks! Homage Subset (1989/1994)

56 The Garden of Peace
57 Late Night Discovery
58 The Last Picture Show
59 Blasted into Oblivion
60 Unspeakable Experiments
61 Flight of the Doomed
62 Last Licks
63 Common Cause
64 Slaughter in the Suburbs
65 Naked and the Dead
66 Earth Triumphant

....

Wally Wood (1927–81)

selected horror comics & magazines checklist (1950–79)

....

BLUE BOLT WEIRD TALES OF TERROR
(1949–53) [Star Publications]
Formerly BLUE BOLT (1940–49)
Becomes GHOSTLY WEIRD STORIES with #120
#118 (Apr 1953) 10¢

BORIS KARLOFF TALES OF MYSTERY
(1963–80) [Gold Key]
Formerly BORIS KARLOFF THRILLER (1962–63)
#9 (Mar 1969) 12¢

CASTLE OF FRANKENSTEIN
(1962–75) [Gothic Castle Publishing]
#10 (Feb 1966) 35¢
#11/v3#3 (1967) 35¢
#18/v5#2 (1972) 60¢
#21/v6#1 (1974) 75¢

CREEPY
(1964–83) [Warren Publishing]
#9 (Jun 1966) 35¢
#38 (Mar 1971) 60¢
#41 (Sep 1971) 60¢
#48 (Oct 1972) $1.00
#55 (Aug 1973) $1.00
#75 (Nov 1975) $1.00
#78 (Mar 1976) $1.00
#87 (Mar 1977) $1.25
#91 (Aug 1977) $1.50
1969 Yearbook (1968) 50¢

THE CRYPT OF TERROR
(1950) [EC Comics]
Formerly CRIME PATROL (1948–50)
Becomes TALES FROM THE CRYPT with #20
#18 (Jun/Jul 1950) 10¢

DARK MYSTERIES
(1951–55) [Master-Merit Publications]
#1 (Jun 1951) 10¢
#2 (Aug 1951) 10¢

EERIE
(1947–54) [Avon Periodicals]
Becomes STRANGE WORLDS with #18
#2 (Aug/Sep 1951) 10¢
#3 (Oct/Nov 1951) 10¢
#4 (Dec/Jan 1952) 10¢
#5 (Feb/Mar 1952) 10¢
#6 (Apr/May 1952) 10¢
#7 (Jun/Jul 1952) 10¢
#16 (Jun/Jul 1954) 10¢
#17 (Aug/Sep 1954) 10¢

EERIE
(1964) [IW Enterprises]
#1 (1964) 10¢
#9 (1964) 10¢

EERIE
(1965–83) [Warren Publishing]
#5 (Sep 1966) 35¢
#11 (Sep 1967) 40¢
#14 (Apr 1968) 40¢
#60 (Sep 1974) $1.25
#61 (Nov 1974) $1.00

FAMOUS FILMS
(1964) [Warren Publishing]
#1 (1964) 35¢
Cover title THE HORROR OF PARTY BEACH

FAMOUS MONSTERS OF FILMLAND
(1958–83) [Warren Publishing]
#58 (Oct 1969) 50¢

Back cover art by Russ Jones and Wally Wood for
Famous Films #1 (1964) Warren Publishing

**FORBIDDEN TALES OF DARK MANSION (1972–
74) [DC Comics]**
Formerly DARK MANSION OF FORBIDDEN
LOVE (1971–72)
#13 (Nov/Dec 1973) 20¢

GHOST MANOR SECOND SERIES
(1971–84) [Charlton Comics]
Cover title VISIT GHOST MANOR
#8 (Nov 1972) 20¢

GHOSTLY TALES
(1966–84) [Charlton Comics]
Cover title GHOSTLY TALES FROM THE
HAUNTED HOUSE
v8#107 (Oct 1973) 20¢

GHOSTS
(1971–82) [DC Comics]
Formerly GHOST (1971)
#2 (Nov/Dec 1971) 25¢
#40 (Jul 1975) 50¢

THE HAUNT OF FEAR
(1950–54) [EC Comics]
Formerly GUNFIGHTER (1948–50)
v1#15 (May/Jun 1950) 10¢

v1#16 (Jul/Aug 1950) 10¢
v2#4 (Nov/Dec 1950) 10¢
v2#5 (Jan/Feb 1951) 10¢
v2#6 (Mar/Apr 1951) 10¢

THE HOUSE OF MYSTERY
(1951–83) [DC Comics]
#180 (May/Jun 1969) 12¢
#183 (Nov/Dec 1969) 15¢
#184 (Jan/Feb 1970) 15¢
#185 (Mar/Apr 1970) 15¢
#189 (Nov/Dec 1970) 15¢
#199 (Jan/Feb 1972) 25¢
#251 (Mar/Apr 1977) $1.00

HOUSE OF SECRETS
(1956–78) [DC Comics]
#91 (Apr/May 1971) 15¢
#96 (Feb/Mar 1972) 25¢

MONSTER WORLD
[Warren Publishing]
aka FAMOUS MONSTERS OF FILMLAND #70
#1 (Nov 1964) 35¢

MYSTERY COMICS DIGEST
(1972–75) [Gold Key]
#1 (Mar 1972) 50¢
#2 (Apr 1972) 50¢

MYSTIC COMICS
(1951–57) [Atlas/Marvel Comics]
#52 (Oct 1956) 10¢

NIGHTMARE
(1970–75) [Skywald Publishing]
V1#1 (Dec 1970) 50¢

RIPLEY'S BELIEVE IT OR NOT!
(1967–80) [Gold Key]
#80 (Aug 1978) 50¢

**RIPLEY'S BELIEVE IT OR NOT! TRUE
GHOST STORIES**
(1965–66) [Gold Key]
#1 (Jun 1965) 12¢

SHOCK SUSPENSTORIES
(1952–55) [EC Comics]
#2 (Apr/May 1952) 10¢
#3 (Jun/Jul 1952) 10¢
#4 (Aug/Sep 1952) 10¢
#5 (Oct/Nov 1952) 10¢
#6 (Dec/Jan 1953) 10¢
#7 (Feb/Mar 1953) 10¢
#8 (Apr/May 1953) 10¢
#9 (Jun/Jul 1953) 10¢

#10 (Aug/Sep 1953) 10¢
#11 (Oct/Nov 1953) 10¢
#12 (Dec/Jan 1954) 10¢
#13 (Feb/Mar 1954) 10¢
#14 (Apr/May 1954) 10¢
#15 (Jun/Jul 1954) 10¢

STARTLING TERROR TALES
(1952–54) [Star Publications]
#10 (1952) 10¢

TALES FROM THE CRYPT
(1950–55) [EC Comics]
Formerly THE CRYPT OF TERROR (1950)
#21 (Dec/Jan 1951) 10¢
#24 (Jun/Jul 1951) 10¢
#25 (Aug/Sep 1951) 10¢
#26 (Oct/Nov 1951) 10¢
#27 (Dec/Jan 1952) 10¢

TALES OF TERROR ANNUAL
(1951–53) [EC Comics]
#1 (1951) 25¢
#2 (1952) 25¢
#3 (1953) 25¢

THIS IS SUSPENSE!
(1955) [Charlton Comics]
Formerly STRANGE SUSPENSE STORIES
(1952–54)
Becomes STRANGE SUSPENSE STORIES with
#27
#23 (1955) 10¢

TOWER OF SHADOWS
(1969–71) [Marvel Comics]
Becomes CREATURES ON THE LOOSE with
#10
#5 (May 1970) 15¢
#6 (Jul 1970) 15¢
#7 (Sep 1970) 15¢
#8 (Nov 1970) 15¢

UNCANNY TALES
(1952–57) [Atlas/Marvel Comics]
#48 (1956) 10¢

THE UNEXPECTED
(1968–82) [DC Comics]
Formerly TALES OF THE UNEXPECTED
(1956–68)
#122 (Dec/Jan 1971) 15¢
#137 (Jul 1972) 20¢
#138 (Aug 1972) 20¢

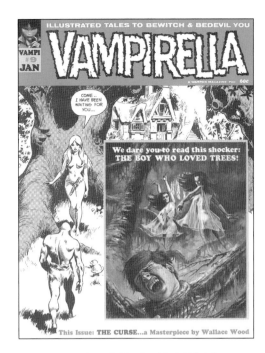

Cover art by Wally Wood and Boris Vallejo for
Vampirella #9 (January 1971) Warren Publishing

VAMPIRELLA
(1969–83) [Warren Publishing]
#9 (Jan 1971) 60¢
#10 (Mar 1971) 60¢
#12 (Jul 1971) 60¢
#19 (Sep 1972) $1.00
#27 (Sep 1973) $1.00
Annual #1 (1972) 75¢

THE VAULT OF HORROR
(1950–55) [EC Comics]
Formerly WAR AGAINST CRIME! (1948–50)
#12 (Apr/May 1950) 10¢
#13 (Jun/Jul 1950) 10¢

WEIRD MYSTERY TALES
[DC Comics]
#23 (Oct 1975) 25¢

WITCHCRAFT
(1952–53) [Avon Periodicals]
#1 (Mar/Apr 1952) 10¢

THE WITCHING HOUR
(1969–78) [DC Comics]
#12 (Jan 1971) 15¢
#15 (Jun 1971) 15¢

Sources

MANY OF the films reviewed within these pages are available from the following video companies:

Alpha Home Entertainment
www.oldies.com
PO Box 101, Narberth, PA, 19072-0101, United States
Phone: 1-800-336-4627, or 1-610-649-7565 for free catalog

Anchor Bay Entertainment
www.anchorbayentertainment.com

Barrel Entertainment
www.barrel-entertainment.com
PO Box 43588, Detroit, MI, 48243, United States
Phone: 1-313-965-3245
Fax: 1-313-965-9600

Image Entertainment, Inc.
www.image-entertainment.com
20525 Nordhoff Street, Suite 200, Chatsworth, CA, 91311, United States
Phone: 1-800-473-3475

Something Weird Video
www.somethingweird.com
PO Box 33664, Seattle, WA, 98133, United States
Phone: 1-888-634-3320
Fax: 1-425-438-1832

Many thanks to those labels who were able to provide me with review copies of their films.

Acknowledgements

SPECIAL THANKS go out to the following individuals and business who were important in the development of this book, whether it be for their input and/or editorial skills, for their allowing me access to their collections and/or to pick their brains, or for their emotional and/or financial support; I couldn't have done it without you:

Devon Bertsch, Bigfoot Comics & Cards, Richard Cardella, Earl Craver, Jackie Currie, Charles Dawson, Laurie Dawson, Dave Drui, The Everett Public Library, Gary's Books & Collectibles, Robert Griffin, Gary Hill, International Movie Database, Brian Jones, Bruce Jones, KIRO-TV, Chuck Lindenberg, Danny Nowak, Xan Nyfors, Scarecrow Video, Tauber Stach, Gerald Stine, Judy Stine, Michael von Sacher-Masoch, and Jack Weaver.

About the Author

WHEN HE'S not moonlighting as a 390 lb. Swedish physicist in low budget horror films, Scott Aaron Stine can be found sitting at his desk, repeatedly bashing his head against the computer monitor.

He is the author of two books devoted to horror films, *The Gorehound's Guide to Splatter Films of the 1960s & 1970s* [McFarland, 2001] and *The Gorehound's Guide to Splatter Films of the 1980s* [McFarland, 2003]. Prior to this, he published numerous magazines, including *Trashfiend* [Stigmata Press, 2002–03], *GICK!* [Stigmata Press, 1998–2001] and *Filthy Habits* [Stigmata Press, 2002–03]. He also published and co-authored *The Trashfiend's Guide to Collecting Videotapes* [Stigmata Press, 2003]. His oft-reprinted article "The Snuff Film: The Making of an Urban Legend," which first appeared in *The Skeptical Inquirer* [CSICOP, May/June 1999], featured in a UK broadcast documentary from Lion Television Ltd.

Under the *nom de plume* of Reginald Bloom, Mr. Stine has had fiction published in such periodicals as *Lovecraft's Weird Mysteries* and *Raw Media Mags*, and in such e-zines as *Crimson, The Art of Horror* and *Chiaroscuro*; his contribution to the latter placed third in the Seventh Chiaroscuro Short Story Contest and was given an honorable mention in *The Year's Best Fantasy & Horror* [St. Martin's Press, 2002]. Most recently, his work appeared in the anthology *Cold Flesh* [Hellbound Books, 2005].

Mr. Stine also writes, performs and produces music for the post-industrial rock outfit Post-Mortem Pre-Op, the instrumental surf band The Deathshead Virgins, the hardcore metal group Cruciform Rust, and the experimental noise project Uhm… His music has been featured on such CD compilations as *41st Street All Stars* [Everott, 2001] and *Seattle Metal Online: Volume Two* [Seattle Metal Online, 2003].

In what passes as a day job, Scott is also a major collector and dealer of vintage memorabilia, selling through his online business of The Trash Collector. (www.thetrashcollector.com)

In his perpetual defense, Mr. Stine adheres to his trademarked adage of "So Many Bad Films… So Few Brain Cells." He currently resides in Everett, Washington.

Index

italics = films, tv shows, publications / 'quotation marks' = short stories & comic strips

A HEADPRESS BOOK

First published by Headpress in 2009

Headpress
Suite 306, The Colourworks
2a Abbot Street
London, E8 3DP, United Kingdom

Tel: 0845 330 1844
Email: headoffice@headpress.com
Web: www.headpress.com

TRASHFIEND
Disposable Horror Fare of the 1960s & 1970s, Volume One

Text copyright © **Mr Scott Aaron Stine**
This volume copyright © 2009 Headpress
Design and layout: **Mr Scott Aaron Stine** & **Mr Joe Scott Wilson**
Front cover elements: Foreground art by Jad from *The Haunt of Horror* v1#3 Sept 74 (Marvel Comics
    Group); Background art from the US lobby card for *La Notte Che Evelyn Usci dalla Tomba* (1971,
    Phase One Films, Inc); Film strip art from the UK novelization of *Squirm* (1976, Sphere Books).
Proofing: **Ms Jennifer Wallis**
Service engineer: **Mr Caleb Selah** / Headpress Diasporas: **Mr David Kerekes, Ms Shelley Lang,
    Mr Thomas Campbell, Ms Bianca Curacao-Nicholls & Mr Dylan Harding**

Images are from the collection of the author unless noted otherwise and are reproduced in this book
as historical illustrations to the text. Grateful acknowledgement is made to the respective artists,
photographers and publishing houses.

British Library Cataloguing in Publication Data
A catalogue record for this book is available from the British Library

ISBN 9781900486668

Printed in Great Britain by the MPG Books Group, Bodmin and King's Lynn